"With decades of on-the-ground leadership in local churches, Doug Dees offers a lifetime of wisdom on making fully formed followers of Jesus. Beyond a weekend seminar, beyond a program, he argues disciple-making is a relational, messy, life commitment that follows the footsteps and model of Jesus. With a rich theological outlook and practical application, I have learned much from Doug. Highly recommended!"

Dr. Heath A. Thomas
President and Professor of Old Testament
Oklahoma Baptist University

"Doug Dees has written an amaz... g, ...n, helpful, and healing book. In one extended metaphor, Dees shows how there can be no jailed Jesus. We try to jail Jesus in church. We try to jail Jesus in doctrine, or in rituals, or in a nation or denomination. But you can't jail Jesus, and this is the best 'Get Out of Jail Free' card I've ever read."

Leonard Sweet
Best-selling author of over 70 books
Charles Wesley Distinguished Professor of Doctoral Studies at Evangelical Seminary
Distinguished Visiting Professor at Tabor College, George Fox University, Drew University
Founder, Spirit Venture Ministries and The Salish Sea Press

"My dear friend Doug does a great job helping all of us understand the struggle in the modern church of accomplishing the great commission. I appreciate his transparency in the journey, along with giving hope that the church can get out of Fish Prison."

Brandon Guindon
Lead Pastor, RealLifeTexas.org
Author, *Disciple Making Culture*
Co-author, *Real Life Discipleship—Training Manual*

FISH PRISON

LIVING BEYOND THE GLASS

DOUG DEES

HIGHERLIFE
PUBLISHING & MARKETING

Fish Prison

Published by HigherLife Development Services Inc.
PO Box 623307
Oviedo, Florida 32762
www.ahigherlife.com

Copyright © 2021 Doug Dees

ISBN: 978-1-954533-16-5 (Paperback)
978-1-954533-17-2 (ebook)
Library of Congress Control Number: 2021905691

No part of this book may be reproduced without permission from the publisher or copyright holder who holds the copyright, except for a reviewer who may quote brief passages in a review; nor may any part of this book be transmitted in any form or by any means, electronic, mechanical, photocopying, recording, or other means without prior written permission from the publisher or copyright holder.

Unless otherwise noted, Scripture quotations are from the HOLY BIBLE, ENGLISH STANDARD VERSION. ® (ESVR), copyright © 2001 by Crossway Bibles, a publishing ministry of Good News Publishers. Used by permission. All rights reserved.

Scripture quotations marked NASB are taken from the NEW AMERICAN STANDARD BIBLE®, copyright © 1960,1962,1963,1968,1971,1972,1973, 1975,1977,1995 by The Lockman Foundation. Used by permission.

Scripture quotations noted NIV are from the HOLY BIBLE, NEW INTERNATIONAL VERSION ®, copyright 1973, 1978, 1984 by Biblica. Used by permission. (www.Lockman.org).

Scripture quotations noted NKJV are taken from the NEW KING JAMES VERSION, copyright 1982 by Thomas Nelson Inc. Used by permission. All rights reserved.

Printed in the United States of America.

10 9 8 7 6 5 4 3 2 1

Contents

Acknowledgments   **vii**

Introduction – My Journey   **1**

ONE The Parable of the Fish Prison   **5**

How We Got Re-imprisoned

The Problems with Helping Fish Find Open Water

TWO Disclaimer. Caution. Structure.   **17**

Why an Aquarium?

Heart Is First

Jesus: The First Prison Breaker

THREE Factory Church   **35**

FOUR The Disciple-Maker Explained   **45**

Fibonacci, Fractal Growth, and God's Reproducing Ideas

FIVE The Three Questions   **57**

Ways to Ask Them

Disciplines. Fruit. Gifts.

Three Questions Relate to the Six Relational Habits

SIX A Deeper Look at the Six Habits   **73**

Habit 1 Finding the Person of God

Habit 2 Immersing in Him

Habit 3 Getting Out Lets Others In

Habit 4 Cultivating Community

Habit 5 Serving Our Circle and Beyond

Habit 6 Going Outside

SEVEN   As You Are Going   **117**

        The Enemy Hates Intentionality

        Staying Beyond the Glass – The Process

        Traits–Exercises–One Anothering

        Terminology

        My Church

        Conclusion

Bibliography   **143**

Acknowledgments

I want to thank my wife Karen for putting up with my odd habits of editing on clotheslines, and early morning shuffling around to write. And to my adult kiddos, Katie and Matt, even though they are well out of the nest, they continue to encourage me. I want to thank my dear friends Mark Lambert, Marvin Burchfield, Chris Malone, Troy Brown, and Gary Lombard for believing in me, and for encouraging me forward.

The inception of this book began twelve years ago when I was at First Orlando. The "three questions" have been a pre-occupation for a decade. But portions of the six habits were shaped by the work we did as a staff at First Moore. After we decided to begin a relational model of disciple-making we wrestled through how to define common language so we could concisely follow a relational vision. It was a great time and I thank all of you.

Lastly my publisher, David Welday, of HigherLife Publishing and for Andrew Ste. Marie for walking me through this process.

Introduction

As you read, I hope and pray you sense God drawing your heart to His, while also hearing ways we may be stuck behind the glass. You may think you hear me saying that all churches in the West are horrible and that everyone in them is completely wrong, and they are all prisons. I am not. There are many bright spots that shine for Christ. But if you are one of those people who are stuck, and you are asking, "Is this really what it's supposed to be like?" then keep reading.

Our Leader does not put His fish in an aquarium.

We do that. We build fish prisons. We sometimes work frantically to maintain them. Our own personal ones, and our religious ones. We keep what is comfortable near us, many times avoiding all else.

If you say you follow Him, pick up a hammer. Those who follow Jesus are to break people out of prison as He did. We must set captives free, just as He did. Isaiah 61:1 and Luke 4:18 tell us that He came "to proclaim liberty to the captives, and the opening of the prison to those who are bound."

He came to set captives free. But are we free? What's containing us? A fish prison? A religious prison or a personal prison or both? "Follow me, I will make you keepers of the aquarium," Jesus did not say. He said, "I will make you fishers of men" (Matt. 4:19).

I'm pointing the above questions at myself. I struggle daily to get beyond the glass of my own prisons. I must.

What does it mean to break the glass? I have to start my own breaking. You yourself must start your breaking. We each can decide to run to God, and increasingly, day by day, become more relationally close to our Heavenly Father, to Jesus our Lord and Savior, and to our guard and guide, the Holy Spirit ... then to help others do the same.

When I started thinking there may be some glass to break I was in what I call "factory church." Not being mean. It just felt that way to me personally. I have been a part of rural churches and mega-churches. Now, don't hear me wrong—I loved those churches and the people who called themselves by His name in all those places. But since I started being a part of leading, I could not get past the nagging feeling that I was running a system and not doing as much loving and relational connecting as I could. I had one of my pastors say this, "There have been many Sundays where I feel like I am pouring my heart out ... I'm up there preaching with a firehose trying to give out living water...and the congregation is sitting out there catching some in thimbles ... and then as they leave ... they trip in the parking lot and spill it." I know that feeling. There were great people I got to minister to and with. But so much of the time I was either worried about numbers or knowledge. I found myself stuck behind the religious glass, as well as the personal glass. "How many did we have?" was the question many times. Or "What are they studying?" "How well do they know it?" "How many classes have they gone through?" These are not bad questions. But they left me hungry for something more.

Years ago I realized I was wanting to answer questions like, "How well are they loving each other?" "Who has come to realize recently how much God loves them?" "How are they loving others beyond the hours they are on this property?" Those questions came from the great commandment ... to love God and love others. In Matthew 22:37-40 God says, "You shall love the Lord your God with all your heart and with all your soul and with all your mind. This is the great and first commandment. And a second is like it: You shall love your neighbor as yourself. On these two commandments depend all the Law and the Prophets." But no one was asking me those questions. Yet I knew my God was asking me to do things beyond the glass, that I just could not seem to fit into my schedule. I found myself more than once feeling like the two guys who walked past the half-dead guy before the good Samaritan came by. "But a Samaritan, as he journeyed, came to where he was, and when he saw him, he had compassion" (Luke 10:33). I just had too much on my plate to slow down ... so I thought. But, since the questions about relationships were rarely if ever asked, I really didn't have to answer them. Right? Even though God was asking them of me, I was too busy answering the other ones. I justified my actions. I was wrong. Again, I'm not saying I was working in bad places. It is just how the system worked. More questions about "how *many* are there?" than "how *well* are they?" The second question was just assumed. We assumed if we gathered, they would get better. Not necessarily true. What is assumed is rarely intentioned. Over the last fifteen years or so many disciple-making churches have emerged, and some significant bright spots of light started shining. God is at work more than we imagine. His work just might not be measured the way we are used to. In fact, that which is most important is hardest to measure.

Also, volume can create problems if you don't focus hard to get people in smaller groups where real relational discipleship can happen. But then you can still have issues. Putting a new relational DNA into an old system of volume measurement can be daunting. New wine in old wineskins kind of a thing. I have experienced that at all levels. So, what you will find in Fish-Prison is what I have come to realize is foundational to spiritual relational health and is needed in a time of failing systems of gathering. I have been a part of the problem. I now want to step up to try to be a small part of the solution. I hope the musings of my journey, and the "three questions" (chapter five) you'll find, will help you follow Him well … and then help you help others do the same.

ONE

The Parable of the Fish Prison

Imagine standing on the bow of a large ship in the vast ocean. Looking out on miles and miles of beautiful open sea. Out there, bobbing around in the water, as far as you can see, are fish tanks—aquariums. Some square. Some round. Some large. Some small.

In the aquariums, are fish. Some alone. Some with other fish.

Are these fish really *in* the ocean? No. They're looking through glass *at* the ocean.

They may want some of the fish who swim by to come get in the aquarium with them or they may want to get out. Those other fish look in and see what? Water which is a little murky. Some fake plastic plants. A motorized life support system which keeps oxygen in the water.

The fish behind the glass need to be fed by someone else. Those fish outside the glass may wonder just what is going on in there. Why would they really want to be a part of it? The fish inside look imprisoned.

Have we forgotten what it means to be free in Christ? Or have we never known?

Have we forgotten what real open water is like? Or have we never known?

Have we become keepers of our aquarium?

We need to be helping fish find open water. Fish can't live free in an aquarium. We, as fish whom Jesus has loved, are to be "open seas fish," loving other fish as we go. As I said in the introduction, we are captives He wants to set free (Isaiah 61:1 and Luke 4:18). But we are no longer captives if we are His. He has set us free.

Yet we have accidently, and also purposely, built for ourselves, aquariums ... personal and religious aquariums.

Yet we have accidently, and also purposely, built for ourselves, aquariums ... personal and religious aquariums.

Much of our lives—and what we call church in America—is spent on ourselves, and in the buildings or programs we have designed to "do church." Sometimes we may attempt to be "fishers of men." Again, Jesus did not say, "Follow me, and I will make you keepers of the aquarium." He said, "I will make you fishers of men."

Though we might know the Bible verses, we don't know the freedom of Mark 4:19. We aren't free. We aren't fishing. We are captives. Maybe re-captives. We became free in Him, then a system guided us into the fish prison.

NOTE: Right about now you are already thinking I am against church. I am not. I am not against church buildings, programs or Sunday mornings. But we have expected the entirety of scripture to happen within these confines—no more than a few hours out of our whole week. And we have sub-divided ourselves into age groups, which can cause us to be unable to know the wisdom of those older in Christ than we are. We have created programs and processes which are to help us grow. This is not all bad, but this is not working as it once did. Unfortunately, some places may look more like a club than a church. This stings me. Does it sting you?

HOW WE GOT RE-IMPRISONED

As I did research for my dissertation, I was looking for writers who saw God, Jesus, and the Holy Spirit as relational, not just rational. Heart and not just mind. A Person, not just a fact of truth. Even in the Spirit's main name He is relational: "The Comforter." In my research I found three men who seemed to be saying what I was sensing: Dr. David Ferguson, Dr. Larry Crabb, and Dr. Neil Anderson. There are many others, but these were the main three at the time. They taught me that the Bible and the God who wrote it are relational first, but also functional and factual.

That was twenty years ago. Many other voices have joined in since then. Bill Hull, in *The Disciple-Making Pastor*, outlines great relational processes. Our staff were greatly influenced by RealLifeDiscipleship.org. Anything you see by that organization has been good to help us move forward. We are grateful for how Jim Putman and Brandon Guindon have been used by God to help so many. Working through the "RealLifeDiscipleship" manual and reading through "DiscipleShift" helped us immensely. These two books can help you make relational discipleship your own wherever you serve in His kingdom.

I realized how many times in church history we have become un-relational and made life in the Spirit very technical, functional, authoritarian, boxed up, or simply a way to keep people in check politically. Martin Luther fought a similar but more deadly fight. We still tend to move toward boxing things up. "Aquarium-ing" them. It is easier to manage. But is that the point? Ease of management? I thank these men, along with many others, who have been working for years to draw us back to the relational God of the Bible.

But let's back up a bit and look at how we possibly got re-imprisoned. In the 1800s, Charles Peirce, the father of Pragmatism, and William James, the Father of American Psychology, both had good intent. In short, their idea was this—think about your thoughts, your plans. Now, what are the outcomes? Pragmatism is basically outcome-based actions. Not bad in and of itself. However, we adopted much of mathematical business pragmatism in the Western church. That type of business pragmatism is basically this. If you wanted to sell ten pieces of product a week, and you had found that for every hundred people you talked to, 10% bought one, then you would need to talk to one hundred people per week to hit your goal of ten sales. This may be fine with sale items, but not with people. You really don't need a God to lead you if you have a plan with outcomes, and a sure-fire way of succeeding numerically. Just go get a hundred people.

> Christ has set life up so we are around people all the time all day who don't know Him, or don't know Him well.

I remember door knocking on evangelism evenings, and then going back to the church building to talk about how many people came to Christ versus how many doors we knocked on. Now, I agree with looking for people who don't know Christ in order to talk to them, befriend them, love them. But if I pay attention to those around me in my daily life, that would give me scores of people to love, and talk to. So why go knock on the door of a stranger? Maybe they were a guest at church and gave you their address. They basically invited you to contact them. And you should. But why not make disciples of those you already know? You know, love your neighbor.

Christ has set life up so we are around people all the time all day who don't know Him, or don't know Him well.

Our problem is we seem to be trying to get to the "sale" too quickly. Or we are scared and won't talk to them at all about God. So we just force ourselves to pick some people and talk. And if they don't "accept" Christ on the first conversation, then why have another one? In my opinion, that is a wrong assumption. If you genuinely cared about someone, and you knocked on their door to talk to them about Christ, and they did not accept your presentation, would you go back? If you cared about them when you were there, did you ask them how you could pray for them? If they said something like their mother was in the hospital, and you said you would pray, why not go back next week to see how their mom was doing? And then go back the next week to check on her. And go back the next week to see if there was anything else you could pray about. That seems loving to me. That would not just be pragmatism, that would be loving.

However, I personally do know people who came to Christ this way. A knock on a door. My point here is that may have been one way, but not the only way. Christ seemed to meet people where they were as He went about life. Relational intentionality, "as you go."

About the same time as Peirce and James introduced Pragmatism, Sigmund Freud, the father of psychoanalysis, in his desire to see people cured of mental and societal issues, acciden-

tally took soul care outside the church. I don't think that was his
intent. There was not really such a thing as a psychologist until
that point. The original psychologists were called "alienists."
They worked with people who had alienated themselves from
society because of their deeply abhorrent behavior. Psychology
has grown over the years, and psychologists help people in
many ways.

Are we trying to fix souls without consulting the maker of souls?

Yet it is the church's job, through the genuine comfort of
the Holy Spirit, to care for one another's souls. But over time
we, the church, have become very pragmatic, looking for bigger numbers and quicker ways to grow numerically large. This
came with a price, at times, of growing large
but growing more spiritually unhealthy. Not
true everywhere, but it seems we were always
comparing numbers, not health. I have at-
tended enough pastors' conferences to know
what one of the first questions is: "So, how
many you runnin' these days?" We compare
ourselves and then feel bad or good based on whether our number is larger. For those who want to argue about this, if our
church growth principles worked, why are they not working
very well now in so many churches in the West? Why is the
church declining so much? A book to read which explains a bit
of this is *The Myth of the Dying Church* by Glenn Stanton. The
church is only dying in some areas, and thriving in others, especially in other countries.

Yes, there are those churches which have a DNR. In life-
or-death situations many people have a pre-decided DNR. Do
Not Resuscitate. In some people's minds and in some churches
it seems we have a spiritual DNR. Do Not Revitalize. It seems

Are we trying to fix souls without consulting the maker of souls?

we only want enough Jesus to get us to our last breath. We don't want more. We really don't want to live for Him. Just with Him, or near others who live for Him. Vicariously living the Christian life. We applaud when someone gets baptized or we hear a good missions report, and we had absolutely nothing to do with it. Not even praying. Nor are we personally doing much to help things move forward. It's like going to an OKC Thunder game and the Thunder wins. People say, "We won." No, the Thunder won. We watched.

We must make certain our growth is based on truth and health, not hype. Christ has asked us to make disciples, not design a comfortable aquarium. The apostles and Paul and Silas did what they did because it was only what Christ had asked them to do. In Acts 17:6 it is recorded that the locals said, "These men who have turned the world upside down have come here also." Has that ever been said of you or your church? We know many came to Christ there, and the church at Thessalonica came into being. Why have we become so obsessed with the size of a congregation and the popularity of a preacher? We have bought into pragmatism too much. We could be asking, "How could we plant a church in a new city where God is calling us?" Think about how God called Paul, then Paul went into the synagogues to teach from the scriptures. Paul knew he was sent.

In a class I once took, Christian psychologist Larry Crabb said, "If we were to relationally disciple one another as we should, we would need far less Christian counselors. Jesus can save our soul, but when it comes to issues of the heart, instead of turning to one another, we pay a hundred dollars an hour to have a friend we can talk to." Please don't think I am disparaging Christian counselors. He wasn't and I'm not. I am so very grateful that they would go through the training and become very skillful at helping souls wrestle through the angst of living on a fallen planet. I have dear friends who are counselors, who have helped me deeply. I wish them well. I wish they could help us all learn how to relate to one another better as the body of Christ. We could learn from them. After all, psychology is the study of the soul. And our great God is the One who created the soul. But could we not learn from one another as part of the church to relationally treat each other well and heal each other's wounds? As I studied in seminary, I realized I was working to see how theology—the study of God—and psychology—the study of the soul—were intertwined. So why not ask the creator of the soul how it should function? At the time this was called integration. But now I see it more as re-integration.

The Maker and the soul must come back together. They should never have come apart. What soul doesn't want a garden walk with a loving Father? But here we are.

We have relied too much on the classroom and sitting in rows, learning with our minds what God wrote for our hearts. Face to face heart talk is needed.

Relational discipleship is what God intended, but somehow we got caught up in re-imprisonment. Christ showed us relational discipleship, and then asked us to do it. We need to take some of that classroom time, sit in small circles and help each other with our souls and our hearts. Yet the mind is more measurable than the heart. We can memorize verses and measure that progress. We can take tests about biblical information. Though not a bad thing to do in school, I'm afraid we have neglected the heart while focusing on the mind. We need both. In many ways we have missed the heart and the soul of Christ's intent.

Someone who is mourning needs me to comfort them, not just explain comfort to them. They do not need me to quote, "We know that God causes all things to work together for good to those who love God, to those who are called according to His purpose" (Rom. 8:28). They need me to be someone who will "mourn with those who mourn" (Rom. 12:15b). We need to take seriously that God, in all His trinitarian-ness, is relational. With Himself first and then with us. He is about loving others and making disciples.

The love which God expresses through Paul is first relational. But we must know that love in order to practice it. We can't replicate that which we do not know. "Love is patient and kind; love does not envy or boast; it is not arrogant or rude. It does not insist on its own way; it is not irritable or resentful; it does not rejoice at wrongdoing, but rejoices with the truth. Love bears all things, believes all things, hopes all things, endures all things. Love never ends" (1 Cor. 13:4-8). Again, in Philippians 1:7-9 Paul tells us, "For it is only right for me to feel this way about you all, because I have you in my heart, since both in my imprisonment and in the defense and confirmation of the gospel, you all are partakers of grace with me. For God is my witness, how I long for you all with the affection of Christ Jesus. And this I pray, that your love may abound still more and more in real knowledge and all discernment." Do we live this way?

Disciples lead with love. Not shallow emotions, but a deep heart-felt love. We can help each other become who and what Christ has asked us to be: Disciple-Makers. Instead of being stuck behind the glass, we must help each other find open water, as well as bring fresh water to our gatherings. It is not so much about ditching what we have as it is converting it, looking at life differently, and living as His disciples in all of it—all our time, in church and out, not just part of it.

THE PROBLEMS WITH HELPING FISH FIND OPEN WATER:

One—*We've become content with fish tank water.*

It's really not water. Often it is recirculated swimming liquid. Sometimes our personal life, and our "church life," are the same every week. Every Sunday. Rarely anything new. We sit in the same rows on the same seats. We intellectually learn things, but our hearts are not changed. We have become content living in the fish tank, and fishing in the fish tank. I had someone recently come up to me and say, "Hey, when are you going to get us some new prospects for our Sunday school class?" In other words, "When are you going to go fishing and come back with a little plastic bag with fish in it and pour them into our tank so we can have more in here?" Wow. Really?

In our past we may have been lied to. Made to feel guilty because we don't have more people in our room. But it is all we know. So we become as comfortable as we can. Questioning whether God is even personal. The enemy is dividing us and containing us. It is the water we know.

Two—*We're afraid, and therefore we won't break the glass.*

We must break the glass. But if we do break it, we think we will let the bad water in, or we will let fish out. Or even worse, let new fish in which are not like us. How will we keep the purity of the fish and the water consistent if we break the glass? Are we overly concerned for the wrong things? Could we keep our high view of scripture and, at the same time, swim around looking for fish who need Jesus? If we can't, we need to adjust our theology and view of scripture. After all, we are supposed to be fishers of men. Our purity is based on Jesus, and how we reveal Him to others as we go, and show them how to follow Him. Not just on Sunday. In a row. In a seat. In a building.

Three—*The worst problem of all ... we don't see the first two as problems.*

The church building is a fine place to meet and worship together. Church gatherings are a time and place to spend time worshiping and disciple-making—being real about who Christ is in us and what Christ instructed us to do. We do need to gather for those purposes. But the building is not the church. I am not suggesting getting rid of your aquarium. Just convert it. Break some of the glass walls. Suggest people live more outside, rather than simply waiting to be back in the building each week. Your time in the building should be the beginning of your week of going beyond the glass, into the life you lead for Him out there—disciple-making. That time should also be for celebrating who God is and what God did while you were out there last week, making a difference in the lives you connected with out there.

You don't have to be stuck behind the glass of your own comfort zone, or that of the religious comfort zone. You can break out. You can become all that He sees you to be. You can make a huge difference in the lives of those around you. You are an ambassador in Christ's kingdom. You will have to drop a lot of preconceived ideas about how relationships with God and others work. But you can break out of your religious aquarium and learn to swim in open water. How are your fish bowls holding you back from following Jesus as He asks? What "fish prison" does He want to help you break out of? What is stopping you?

If you are inside the fishbowl, good news ... God is still working to get Matthew 4:19, "to make you fishers of men," accomplished in the lives of those who will follow Him. If you did not grow up in church, you saw it from the other side of the glass, and the same good news applies. He wants to set you free, and to help you help others get free!

TWO

Disclaimer. Caution. Structure.

Before you start questioning your own fishbowl experience, and structure a strategy to get out, I want you to do two things:

One, put the whip down. Too often, when we start to see God in a new light, we allow the enemy to convince us to whip ourselves for our past. Tell the enemy to go visit his own hometown. That would be hell.

Two, pause and focus on having an "open mindset" and developing a few "relational habits."

DISCLAIMER:

Behind the glass, too much of the time we think life is about us. Our preferences. Our comfort. The way we want to "do church," or "live our personal lives." As we learn to live beyond the glass, life will have more of the substance we actually desire. It can be less random, and more connected. Less painted by the numbers, and more vibrant. Maybe less planned. You may sense some frustration at yourself for what you have done in the past. I felt that way as I realized more and more of what God wanted. I started spiritually demeaning myself for lost opportunities. He drew me out of that tailspin. He can help you too. What you will not find in this book are suggestions that you were completely wrong, or that I have it all figured out. What you will find is a relational set of "three questions" (chapter five) which are focused on the Father, the Son, and the Spirit. These are not the only questions to ask, but are the beginning questions to ask. You will find "six relational habits" which should actually *become* habits in your life in order to develop the spiritual disciplines, spiritual fruit, and spiritual gifts you need to help your life function as God intends.

Too much of the time as individuals we tend to settle on a pattern of life that works. We get by. We make it through another day. As a church, we settle on a process or program that seems to work. By "work" I mean we may see a small numerical increase. These days we see more decrease than increase. Very little spiritual health. Very little reproduction of disciples. I am suggesting you take this relational model, which may be new to you and plug it into your life and your church. This relational model of three questions and six habits can be used to change and connect ourselves even more to the One, the Three, the Trinity, who know us. You will need to work out the questions and habits in your own context. Come up with your own words and phrases. But keep the focus on Him and others. I'm suggesting that you adjust the process and make it what God wants in your life, for health and real spiritual maturity, to the point of reproducing your life. Christ desperately wants to disciple each of us. The Spirit yearns to guide us in that.

Hopefully this book will help you live relationally connected to all three parts of the Trinity, as well as with those where He has placed you—in your family, your work, your community, your church. As you read, let me remind you, the enemy will try to give you thoughts that I am against the life you have now, the gathering of the church, and a certain denomination or non-denomination. I'm not. What I am frustrated with is a tepid life so many believers in America have settled for. I am frustrated with church leadership (myself included) which has allowed nominal Christianity in church as normal. I want us to ask Jesus what He means when He says, "As you go, make disciples."

When we gather (and we must gather regularly) we should be about relational connection based on the Trinity. The three questions and the six relational habits will help. If these are not good reasons for gathering, then why are we gathering? Christ asked us to make disciples who make disciples. So how is that working? Some of you, right now, are saying "Good, we are talking about disciple making." Some of you are saying, "I don't really know what that is. I was hoping this would help me with my confused personal life."

Why can't it be both—helping you personally and helping you become a disciple maker? If you can be more alive in Christ, you could probably help someone else to become more alive in Christ. Shouldn't that be church or disciple-making?

CAUTION:

Treat the following paragraph as potential police tape at a crime scene. Try not to cross this line: Do not immediately allow your thoughts to move toward organization, measurement, and metrics. These are not bad. They are not a crime. But we often start with numerical measuring, programs, and metrics for our lives and for our churches. We have unfortunately been measuring some of the wrong things first, while not really being concerned about the most important things.

I want you to avoid the tendency to immediately start to organize and begin thoughts on metrics or how to numerically measure. Allow yourself to relax. Be one who is related to the God of this universe. Break out of the fish prison. Develop an ever-deepening relationship with God and others. Create habits which enable these relationships to flourish.

Yes, it is a bit of a *relational how-to*. But not necessarily a how to numerically measure success.

I had someone ask me once about measuring. They wanted to know some metrics about a particular ministry. In a bit of frustration, I thought, "I'll bet if you had me growing carrots, you would ask me each week to dig them up and measure them. You have to let the carrots grow." I never said it out loud, but it definitely crossed my mind.

If you are like me, you have already thought about the three and the six ... three questions, and six habits. Two numbers right there for you to start measuring how you are doing at those three questions and the six habits. These are not as linear and measurable as you might think. They are not measurable in traditional ways of time and sequence. They are about re-lationships. So when we get to them in a few chapters, try to enjoy hearing the glass break in your fish prison, as you become a non-captive, and are set free by Jesus Himself. I have had to do this myself. At times it was painful. Other times it was amaz-ingly joyful. I know that drawing nearer to my God as Father, Son, and Holy Spirit is what He wants.

STRUCTURE:
First—The first half of the book walks us through—how we got

here, why we got here, and what I think has been obvious all along (but we have missed).

It seems obvious now, but I have missed it most of my life. It was a small part of what I was doing. But it was not the main reason or the basis. Systems and control and outcome had become the central points of my life. The beginning part of the Old Testament has a lot of system and control. Jesus Himself turned that system upside down and backwards. He made it relational. Men tend to want to focus on structure and control. The priestly system of the Old Testament was not bad. God set it up. It was men who turned it into a pharisaical system—which was way too precise for the sake of being precise. They heaped more on men than God intended. It became about system, not the reasons for the system. Precise is not bad. But precise for the sake of precise misses the point. Control is not bad. But control for the sake of control misses the point. The Levitical law, and the priestly system, and feasts and festivals were not bad. God had meaning behind them. But the meaning became clouded, and then lost, for most.

I have tried to put the intent of this book in the simplest form: Get past overly focusing on systems, processes, and order for your life and church, and focus on Three Persons. I know it is basically a loose system, but I'm not sure of any other way to present it. When I myself look at a list, there is always the first thing listed. As followers of Christ, there was a first thing for us. Jesus said, "No man comes to the Father but by Me." So, experientially, we entered the relationship with the Trinity by One Person. There was an order. Yet prior to that coming to pass, there were, and always have been, Three in One. So, there is some order. But I ask you to try not to overly-order it all.

Second—God Himself uses story to explain Himself and

His ways to us. So, the second half of the book will have much more story and less teaching structure. The "deeper look" has stories of what this feels like. As you read, I pray God brings stories to your mind. Connections with Him and His ways from your past. Instances where you missed Him. Instances where you found Him near. I hope and pray you find a deeper connection with Him, and that you can share that with others in such a way that they do too.

Relax and hear the glass break.

WHY AN AQUARIUM?

One day I caught myself staring through the glass. I was wondering just what those folks not in church thought of us, and how boxed up we seem to have everything. We say we are free in Christ. But it sure did not feel that way to me. I felt like I may have been a captive who was set free, only to get caught again. Trapped behind glass is all some of us have ever known. So an aquarium came to mind. That was quite a few years ago. I wanted more than the personal or religious aquarium. I just didn't know what that might look like.

If I hadn't started breaking glass, I would have continued to adjust to the pain of comfortable-ness ... assuming there is no way out.

If I hadn't started breaking glass, I would have continued to adjust to the pain of comfortable-ness ... assuming there is no way out.

We assume there is no water on the other side of the glass, that we would die out there. But, in the reality of who Jesus is, there is water—living water. Behind the glass as well as beyond the glass, there is hope in Him. But have we settled for less than

Him? I think the answer is yes. And I think the three questions can change that for you, as well as for your church.

Are you willing to ask three questions daily? (Go ahead and look at the beginning of chapter five for the three questions.) Are you willing to follow Him, and the rest of the Trinity, regardless of your circumstances? Scary question, but better than the pain of comfortable-ness. Again, Matthew 4:19 doesn't say, "Follow me and I will make you keepers of the aquarium." Or keepers of the comfort zone. But it might as well. So much of the Western church is stuck behind the glass of our fish prison. Our aquarium is safe and secure from all alarm. I think we have quit leaning on Jesus. We seem to lean on our own finesse and ability to keep safe behind the glass.

Change starts with having a deepening relationship with all three parts of the Trinity. As C.S. Lewis says about Aslan, "He is not safe, but He is good."[1] All three Persons are good, but at times not safe. All three have a coordinated desire to see you become who They see you to be. All three have the same desire to see your heart turn to Them. All three want to see you follow Their lead as you move and breathe daily in the part of the kingdom you occupy. Daily. Moment by moment.

I have been part of the problem and did not know it. Sometimes I am still part of the problem. I have thought way too much in my life about how the aquarium is doing, and not about how the kingdom is doing. Instead of asking, "Are the fish healthy and reproducing?" I would simply count how many were there. During those times, was I actually making disciples of my Lord Jesus Christ? I think I was, but only for a very little portion of my time. I have lived much of my life behind the glass trying to figure out how to get beyond the glass.

---

[1] C.S. Lewis, *The Lion, the Witch and the Wardrobe* (New York: HarperCollins, 1950).

Again, there is hope. There are church families which are getting it done. They are making disciples who make disciples—just like Jesus asked us to do.

The three relational questions are like an adrenaline shot designed to get your heart going again no matter where you are. No matter what glass you are behind. They give energy to what is already there. That energy comes not from the questions, but from the Ones of whom you ask the questions. These questions are not intended to replace a Bible study, a worship time, or a particular ministry. They are to give a Bible study energy and a relationally intentional focus that drives you beyond the study. The three questions, along with the six habits, can be used to focus any ministry of the church back to the basic tenets of disciple-making. If a men's or women's ministry is only about men's or women's topics, you are stuck on topics. Not bad, but not enough. If a men's ministry is about men's topics and disciple-making, it has more life. It is then reproducible. Support groups, also, can fall in on themselves unless they get beyond support.

Too much of the time we have relied on mind and not heart. We need both. Rational over relational leads us toward Pharisaism. And relational without rational can lead to emotionalism.

Again, many of us in the West are too accustomed to the water in our aquarium—the processes, and procedures, and programs, which are only done on certain days and in certain ways. The enemy's sleight of hand has redirected us away from the life-giving spiritual relationships that matter. He has moved us just enough that we didn't notice the drift. We drifted. We shifted. The enemy moves us from function to form. We worry about form, and forget the reason, the function. We have also then relied much on rational thought and information instead of developing relational hearts which cause transformation.

Too much of the time we have relied on mind and not heart. We need both. Rational over relational leads us toward Pharisaism. And relational without rational can lead to emotionalism.

We don't want either of those results. But it seems we have settled for information about God, rather than a deep relationship with God. In the aquarium I found myself settling for processes and programs to grow the church. Isn't church growth supposed to be His doing? He asks us to make disciples. That is our part. Process and program do not make disciples … disciples make disciples. But I have tended to focus more on the process than the person. We are to love Him, love others, and make disciples. The Great Commandment and Great Commission tell us that: Matthew 28:18-20; Matthew 22:37-40. I'm afraid we have slowly moved away from these two greatest expectations. He told us. Jesus Himself said these words. We need to get back to the heart of what He asked. That will involve the three questions as we develop deepening relationships with all three Persons of the Trinity.

> For me, it starts with three spiritually relational questions we ask the Trinity every day, all day, and especially on Sunday.

For me, it starts with three spiritually relational questions we ask the Trinity every day, all day, and especially on Sunday. And it starts with heart.

HEART IS FIRST

Almost every time you see heart and mind in the biblical text, they are in that order. Heart is first. So we are to use them in that order. But we have focused so much on the classroom version of engaging our minds in the written biblical text that we may have missed the fact that our Father starts with the heart. "Trust in the Lord with all your heart, and do not lean on your own understanding. In all your ways acknowledge him, and he will make straight your paths" (Prov. 3:5-6). Heart is first. Second is not leaning on our own understanding, followed by acknowledging Him—relational. Heart and mind are together, in that order, and not separated. After spending so many years in rational thoughts about our Father, many of us know things about Him, while not knowing Him from our heart. "You will seek me and find me, when you seek me with all your heart" (Jer. 29:13). It was true for Israel, and it true for us.

I have missed His heart much of the time in the past. When I am away from home, I try to call or FaceTime with my wife Karen. It is great to hear her voice and see her face. But as I go to sleep it is not the same as having her next to me. It is like having a picture of her on her pillow. Not the same. We treat God similarly when we approach Him with our minds and church processes only, but no depth of heart relationship.

When we miss the most important part, the heart, it is not just sad, it is ineffective. Romans 10:9-10 conveys that we believe with our heart and our mind. But do we? Do we believe Him with our hearts? "For with the heart one believes and is justified, and with the mouth one confesses and is saved." The two passages before this one list mind first, then heart. Yet, it is in our heart that we believe. One of the biggest problems I think we westerners have is this: It is easier to measure mind, process, programs, events, and attendance. It is very hard to measure the heart. It is tough to measure someone becoming more kind.

But you know it when you see growth in kindness, in love, in joy, in peace (Gal. 5:22).

We are to love the Lord our God with all of our heart, soul, and mind—the Great Commandment. In every passage Jesus says this, heart is first and mind is third. Do not assume I am suggesting ditching your mind. I am not. You must connect your mind to what He has said. But if you do not engage your heart, you have disobeyed the Great Commandment. Without the heart, we can become process-only. We can descend to the point of being Pharisees. And with only the heart and not a connected mind, we can be cast adrift and follow any emotionally charged statements we hear. That would cause us to have no "heart-truth" to judge them against. In Ephesians 4:13-14 God says, "Until we all attain to the unity of the faith and of the knowledge of the Son of God, to mature manhood, to the measure of the stature of the fullness of Christ, so that we may no longer be children, tossed to and fro by the waves and carried about by every wind of doctrine." Our deep knowledge of God (not just mind knowledge) will keep us from being wishy-washy believers.

Don't disconnect your mind, but engage your heart. A car with an engine and no transmission is worthless. And vice versa.

Maybe you are asking, "We have to have training to do this, don't we?" Many attempts at training fail. Trying to quickly mass-produce a "one-of-a-kind disciple" falls in on itself, bringing more disillusionment and failure than success. Heart takes time. Attempting to "train disciples" rather than "make disciples" is about as successful as learning to swim by watching YouTube. It may be helpful, but there is no way to feel the water and that sinking in the deep end sensation. Engaging your heart with God and then with another person takes time. But changed hearts change culture.

JESUS – THE FIRST PRISON BREAKER

God in a man's body. That is imprisonment.

But God chose to be born, to become a man, and to dwell among us. He chose imprisonment. Why? So that He could break us out. That is the ultimate aquarium, a small human body imprisoning God. God said through Isaiah the prophet:

> The Spirit of the Lord God is upon me,
> Because the Lord has anointed me
> To bring good news to the afflicted;
> He has sent me to bind up the brokenhearted,
> To proclaim liberty to captives
> And freedom to prisoners. (Isaiah 61:1 NASB)

For Him to set captives free, He first had to start the prison break-out ... to break some of the religious aquarium rules. As soon as His baptism was over the Spirit descended on Him like a dove. Later, He was led by that same Spirit into the wilderness. Forty days of fasting. And we would all guess there was an enormous amount of quiet time listening to His Father. Then the enemy—Satan himself—attempted to imprison Christ forever by trying the same thing Satan did in the garden ... lying. The enemy spoke to Christ, misquoting what God had said. Jesus passed through that test by letting Satan know *exactly* what God had said. It is important to know exactly what God said— that is the reason we start with His Word as Relational Habit Number One, as you will see.

But this wasn't His first brush with imprisoned living. He

was born into captivity in an oppressive world where the governmental system was very dictatorial. The prevailing religious system was incredibly regulated and systematic. A prison in itself. Those living without God were imprisoned by the enemy. And the religious leaders—who were supposed to be there to point to God, had set up their own version of prison. Religious prison. The relationship with God had been missing from that system for many years.

Jesus was planning a prison break. He had to start the break Himself before He could truly break us out. He says,

> Truly, truly, I say to you, he who does not enter the sheepfold by the door but climbs in by another way, that man is a thief and a robber. But he who enters by the door is the shepherd of the sheep. To him the gatekeeper opens. The sheep hear his voice, and he calls his own sheep by name and leads them out. When he has brought out all his own, *he goes before them*, and the sheep follow him, for they know his voice. A stranger they will not follow, but they will flee from him, for they do not know the voice of strangers. (John 10:1-5 emphasis mine)

The line that strikes me is, *He goes before us.* He is the One who leads. He went first. Three years of showing twelve men how to disciple, "as they go." Then the cross and the empty tomb finished the break-out. He had then done all He was to do ... this time (smile).

But let's back up a bit. You may have read about Jesus as a child.

When did Mary, Jesus' mother, tell Him who He was? Did

she and Joseph, His earthly dad, ever talk to Him about the
visits from the angels? How long did Mary ponder those things
in her heart? When did Jesus begin to recognize He was different—that He was God? When did it come to His mind that the
prophet Isaiah was talking about Him (Isa. 61)? We know He
taught well in the temple. He asked great questions even at the
age of twelve. After going back to find Him in Jerusalem, Mary
and Joseph "found him in the temple, sitting among the teachers, listening to them and asking them questions. And all who
heard him were amazed at his understanding and his answers.
And when his parents saw him, they were astonished" (Luke
2:46-48).

Jesus followed the customs of Israel for 30 years. We have
no record of where He taught and what He did for a living,
only that Joseph, his dad, was a carpenter, a stone mason. We
assume Jesus did some of what His father did. Then there was
that fateful day not long after His baptism and the forty days in
the wilderness. It was His custom to go the synagogue on the
Sabbath. In Nazareth, where He grew up, Jesus read from Isaiah 61. When did He know this passage was about Him? That it
was He who would set captives free? Luke records the moment
He said it out loud:

> And the scroll of the prophet Isaiah was given to
> him. He unrolled the scroll and found the place where
> it was written, "The Spirit of the Lord is upon me, be-
> cause he has anointed me to proclaim good news to the
> poor. He has sent me to proclaim liberty to the cap-
> tives and recovering of sight to the blind, to set at liberty
> those who are oppressed, to proclaim the year of the
> Lord's favor." And he rolled up the scroll and gave it

back to the attendant and sat down. And the eyes of all in the synagogue were fixed on him. And he began to say to them, "Today this Scripture has been fulfilled in your hearing." (Luke 4:17-21)

This was a "drop the mic," or scroll, moment.

He had followed God. He had followed what was written, even to this point, when He said, "This scripture is fulfilled." However, at that moment, all hell broke loose. Literally. Game on. A few verses later, "All in the synagogue were filled with wrath. And they rose up and drove him out of the town and brought him to the brow of the hill on which their town was built, so that they could throw him down the cliff. But passing through their midst, he went away" (Luke 4:28-30).

Jesus simply moved on.

From that moment on, He continued to do what His Father asked, as He had in the past. But He had painted a much bigger target on Himself. It is one thing to know you are God; it is a whole other thing to say it out loud!

He had been obedient up to that moment. But that day was different. He declared that He was going to set captives free. He declared He was the Messiah.

He immediately started doing what He said, setting captives free. Many did not like it. They had a system set up to keep people captive. They had their own aquarium—and, for those leaders, it was working quite fine thank you very much. But the ones He came to set free were elated! In the gospel accounts, Jesus then chose disciples, going from city to city and showing them how to make disciples "as you go."

He was a dangerous rebel according to the religious leaders:

He said *what* He shouldn't.

He talked to *whom* He shouldn't.

He helped *when* He shouldn't.

He healed *when* He shouldn't.

He healed *whom* He shouldn't.

He ate *when* He shouldn't.

He ate *what* He shouldn't.

He ate *with whom* He shouldn't.

He ate *where* He shouldn't.

He *went* where He shouldn't.

He *talked to women* He shouldn't.

He *touched* an outcast He shouldn't.

He *let* an outcast touch Him when He shouldn't.

He *healed* those he shouldn't because the leaders called them condemned.

He *went near dead people* when He shouldn't.

He was religiously unclean, and …

He didn't ceremonially wash when He should have.

Over time He probably broke every rule the Pharisees had. But He broke none of God's.

Over time He probably broke every rule the Pharisees had. But He broke none of God's.

He fulfilled all of God's commandments while breaking their man-made commandments. Their man-made commandments prevented people from following God's commands. Jesus had no regard for their commands, but He followed God's command to love others. He even restated it Himself when asked what the greatest commandment was. "You shall love the Lord your God with all your heart and with all your soul and with all your mind. This is the great and first commandment. And a second is like it: You shall love your neighbor as yourself. On these two commandments depend all the Law and the Prophets" (Matt. 22:37-40).

Basically, He took a hammer and broke the glass of the prison that the leaders had constructed to keep an orderly religion. He broke Himself out of their prison, then went about setting a bunch of captives free. Just like He said He would. That scripture was fulfilled. And He was fulfilling it. Daily.

> **Mankind has a knack for putting everything nice and neatly in a box.**

I know this next statement may be a little sacrilegious. But I wonder if He had a little notebook with all the Pharisees' extra laws. Over six hundred of them. I wonder if, when He got up in the morning He thought, "I'm gonna break numbers 12, 28, 386, and 87 today." Actually, He went about His day paying no mind to them, only to His Father, and His Father's desire.

Jesus was raised in a fishbowl religious system. All perfectly contained. Lots of extra rules, but no God as a part of it. Yet Christ was there. In the middle of it as He changed it.

Mankind has a knack for putting everything nice and neatly in a box.

We box things up. A performance box. An accomplishment box. Over the years religious leaders have continued to do that, creating religious containers. As followers of Jesus Christ, we cannot live that way and truly follow Him. Our Leader sets captives free.

THREE

Factory Church

For one chapter let's back up. Let me again tell you how I got where I am. "Factory church" is what I called it. No one said that to me. If you get mad, get mad at me alone. It was really not intended to be factory church. It is what I grew up in. It is just how it felt to me. So, whether it is the murky water you grew up in, or you looked at it from the outside in. It was what it was.

I have ventured beyond the glass numerous times only to go back. I knew from the church I grew up in no one really meant it to be that way, or to feel that way. We had a great youth group, and some of the greatest Sunday School leaders you could ever want. I knew they loved me. We just never talked about it. We talked about God, but it was in a factual, informational, distant sort of way.

Worship was very predictable down to the minute. There was a preciseness to it all. It was the way we did things. It felt like factory church to me. It was not wrong. The leaders did not intend it to be a factory; it just seemed that way sometimes. It is what our leaders were taught to do by those who taught their leaders. And they taught us. And we did it. And people found Jesus, grew to maturity, and then helped others. We were charged to do certain things at certain times in certain ways. And it worked because factory church worked. Sort of. It was very departmentalized. Each department of the factory worked on its own part, hoping the other departments did their jobs. It did not quite feel disjointed because it was what we knew and grew up in. There were systems which worked independently of each other, but for the most part, they worked alongside each other. However, I do remember there was an underlying competition for recognition, volunteers, and dollars. That was not good. It was like the human body if the respiratory system would compete with the digestive system which was arguing with the nervous system. They really ought to work together for the common good of the body. To quote myself from *reSymbol*, "When we piecemeal our church structure in an attempt to make us look like the best parts of all the other churches we want to look like, we end up with the bride of Frankenstein, not the bride of Christ. Frankenstein was barely alive, didn't communicate very well, and all the villagers wanted to kill him."[2]

At that time, our Western society seemed to create—for the most part—people who were not anti-Christian. Most everyone I knew wanted to be a good moral person by societal standards. Many of our collective social norms were much like the church norms. *Andy Griffith* and *Leave It to Beaver* and all that. The societal soup we all grew up in was very similar.

Then for some reasons, which others can explain better than I can, things changed. Society became only "tolerant" of church … and then became "less tolerant" of church … then "frustrated" at church. Now some are increasingly "hostile" to church—and to anyone calling themselves a Christian. And yet

---

[2] Doug Dees, *'reSymbol'* (Orlando: HigherLife Publishing) 2009. P. 44,45.

as I meet new guests coming to our church these days, I find many—as well as those who are already part of our church—are desiring more deeply caring relationships with those who can help them walk through life. So many are not looking just for a spot to be on Sunday, or a process to be part of. They are looking for friends who care about becoming a better person and more genuine as they follow Christ and help others.

In the midst of a societal crumble, a heartfelt need for real, genuine relationships has emerged. They are looking for real friends.

In the past I think we have spent way too much time over-organizing something which by nature is supposed to be more relational, free and fluid. That is church. Were we trying to create the perfect aquarium? The Spirit of God moves as He sees fit. We do not necessarily move the Spirit of God to function for us. But "factory church" worked for a while. Then the numeric decline started. I think this is why Henry Blackaby's book *Experiencing God* was so timely. One of His statements was, "See where God is working, and go work with Him." He also said, "You can't stay where you are and go with God."[3] These statements went against the motto we see in much of western culture: "God, I am working here, come grow what I want to do. I want numeric growth, and spiritual growth too, of course."

God does not seem to always have a pragmatic plan, just relational intents. He knows how it all ends and will bring it to that end. But He is doing that relationally. There are instances where men have influenced God because of their great desire

[3]Henry T. Blackaby, Claude V. King, *Experiencing God* (1990), Back cover, 127.

for His name or for others. Think about Moses not wanting to
see the nation of Israel wiped out. He was concerned about
God's name and the people He loved (Num. 14:13). Matthew
wrote about a woman who persisted for the healing of her
daughter (Matt. 15:28). In both instances they were concerned
about someone else, not themselves. Both relational.

For over a century, the church in the West became more
functional and less relational. It seems like it was more relational in the early 19th century—or even in the agrarian society
where people depended on each other so much. But from the
end of the last century until now, it appears people are becoming hungry for real relationships. The church had turned into
a "place and time," with information and attendance measure-
ments showing that the larger the crowd the better. Meanwhile,
people grew hungrier. Too much of the time a church is measured by its size, not its health.

The factory church began to have fewer raw materials to
work with. Fewer and fewer people came through the doors
simply because it used to be expected by society. The peak of
church attendance in the American church was in about 2009.
If you did not attend regularly, you sure as heck made it there
on Christmas and Easter. Even that has changed.

This is not a slam on all churches. There are some churches
doing just fine. They are making disciples and people are coming to Christ. Their building is a place for meeting and relating,
for learning and growing in Christ, for helping others to do the
same. But much of what they are to do as disciples is beyond the
church campus, out of their normal comfort zone. Beyond the
glass of religion or their own personal aquarium.

For too long, we have defined ourselves by our labels, our
processes, our denominational tendencies, and our factory

names. We have been more concerned about being _____ (add your denominational name) than we have been about being followers of Christ: Disciples who are disciple makers. We call ourselves Christians—though that word is used only three times in the New Testament. Yet we are not doing very well at the last thing Christ asked us to do as His followers: go and make disciples. He asks us to be disciple makers, not attenders.

Factory church is, in many cases, a church about attendance, activity, and information. The growing churches I know of today are churches which are about intentional relationships. That doesn't mean we ditch information or quit using our minds. Biblical information needs to be delivered many times in a relational format, with people who care and will help someone grow.

We have focused on being the church as an organization which manufactures Christians. Way too much of the time, we see the organization—manufacturing processes and procedures and buildings—as the church. This could not be further from what the Father, Jesus, and the Holy Spirit intended. The factory must become a relational culture. This past culture of "Sunday church-dom" or the "entertainment feel of some ways of worship" is not biblically correct. When Jesus asked that we go be disciple-makers, He had no such things in mind that are much of what we currently call church. Our studies and sermons and worship songs can and should be focused on Him. Absolutely. But those few hours total in the building make up less than two percent of your week. What then do you do with the rest of your week? Our weekend study and worship times must celebrate (in spirit and truth) who He is, and what He has done last week in the lives we live. They must anticipate what He will do in our lives next week. Otherwise we have missed the point of looking to Him and following Him. The connected-ness beyond Sunday will increase if we are willing to help people grow in Him. This is not a slam, but a shift that must occur.

In *Canoeing the Mountains*, Tod Bolsinger states, "Christian leaders; You were trained for a world that is disappearing."[4] He is correct. Most of us were trained to manage an organization, not relate to a living organism. In *The Myth of the Dying Church*, Glenn Stanton comments similarly.[5] My compiled paraphrased understanding of their insight is this:

- One—measuring attendance is only one way to measure and is not the best way to measure the health of a church.
- Two—measuring new ways with old measuring sticks is impossible.

If you previously used a yard stick to measure feet, but now you are measuring the volume of water and the flow rate, the stick is useless. Lance Witt in *Replenish* rightly says, "In the contemporary Western church, the shift had moved from the groom to the bride. From Christ to the church. Yet Christ is to be center stage."[6] We need to move Him back. In too many ways, we have slowly moved the church and programs in front of Christ—or we have moved Him to the side. Instead of a deepening relationship with Christ being the center, we are

> If we took a spiritual selfie, Christ would almost be crowded out of the picture with all that we have going on.

---

[4] Todd Bolsinger, *Canoeing the Mountains* (Downers Grove, IL: InterVarsity Press, 2015), 18.

[5] Glen Stanton, *The Myth of the Dying Church*, (Nashville: Worthy Books, 2019).

[6] Lance Witt, *Replenish*, (Grand Rapids: Baker Books, 2011) Ch. 14.

focused on some metrics alone. We need to move Him back to center stage.

If we took a spiritual selfie, Christ would almost be crowded out of the picture with all that we have going on.

He must be the One who disciples us and asks us to do the same with others.

We tend to try to measure everything in a factory church. Sociologist William Bruce Cameron said, "Not everything that counts can be counted, and not everything that can be counted, counts." Listen closely. Most of what can't be measured is what counts the most. Something as simple as someone becoming more kind, because their character is becoming more like Christ. We can see it in their life. But it is quali-fy-able, not quantify-able. I am not saying the factory did not work or did not change lives. Over the years, though, too many of us have just slid into us doing factory work in the factory. Service became a project, not a lifestyle. Worship was what happened on Sunday morning, not a deep connection with our Father. Fellowship was something we did quarterly as a Sunday School class. Evangelism was a presentation we learned, not relationships we developed to see friends come to Christ. It just seemed to be about actions, and steps we dutifully carried out, with very little relationship in them. And we wonder why things are not growing healthily. We who are leaders must lead differently. Again, in *Canoeing the Mountains*, Tod Bolsinger does a great job of explaining how: "If

> There are times I wonder, with all of the online posts of our church activities, does Christ feel like He has to photobomb to get in the picture?

you are going to scale the mountains of ministry, you need to leave behind the canoes and find new navigational tools."[7]

These programmed actions seem to have taken the place of Christ at the center of our lives, and of the Trinity guiding us. Christian life has become functional rather than relational. We need to ask God to breathe life into our activities or we need to stop doing them the way we are doing them.

There are times I wonder, with all of the online posts of our church activities, does Christ feel like He has to photobomb to get in the picture?

That is painful to say. I know. As I have said, I have been part of the problem. Yet Christ is not the kind of King who would force His way into a picture. But He knocks. He waits. He patiently waits for us to realize that we do not have Him in focus. We may not even have Him in the picture.

We must be followers beyond the walls of the church. We must break the stained glass which we may have painstakingly assembled.

To move forward, disciples will need to choose to live beyond the glass of the Fish Prison we have created.

We must be followers beyond the walls of the church. We must break the stained glass which we may have painstakingly assembled.

Much more of our lives can be about genuine fellowship as a lifestyle. It must be about living the love of the gospel in front of people. Intentionally developing a deeper relational connection with our Father. Spiritual health as a lifestyle is imperative for the spiritual growth of a group of people. All of that is collectively a big shift. But it is possible. *To break out of Fish Prison, we must move from inviting people to church to investing in people's lives outside the church.*

---

[7] Bolsinger, back cover.

Strangely enough, that sentence is not even theologically correct. The word for church in the New Testament is ecclesia. It means the "called out ones." The word ecclesia was never used in the Bible to describe a place or a time. It was about a people who lived their lives differently. The closest statement we have to that word defining a place is from Acts 5:42 (NASB): "And every day, in the temple and from house to house, they kept right on teaching and preaching Jesus as the Christ." The "they" is the church. The "called out ones." Every day they talked about Him, in their houses as well as their meeting places. To sit with friends and talk about Jesus, His word, His Father and the Spirit, and how they are changing our lives. Is this not discipleship?

And yes, they lived nearer to each other then. Not like the spread-out cities we live in today. And the temple court was open all the time. Jesus said in the great commission, "As you

> **To break out of FishPrison, we must move from inviting people to church to investing in people's lives outside the church.**

go." In that one phrase He covered all places and all times and all people. We have no excuse. We are the church. We must go to them. I hope you try to move from factory church to what I think Christ is asking of us. But know this, if you do try changing some things inside the fishbowl, you may see some fish start to bite you or each other.

I'm afraid we have gotten away with doing the least He has asked, instead of the most He has asked.

Right about now you may be thinking, "I thought we were also going to talk about our personal comfort zone ... a personal aquarium?" We are. As we get into the three questions you will see how you, as an individual, can be part of the solution in your own personal aquarium, and then also be a part of the solution in the larger religious aquarium.

There is an old story of a dad who had his six-year-old boy at his office while his wife was out. The dad still had some work to finish up before they could head home for the day. The little boy kept wanting to talk and chat with the dad. But the dad needed just a few more minutes to work. So, to keep the boy occupied, the dad grabbed a newspaper he had (I said it was an old story). On one page was an advertisement with a huge picture of the world taken from space with all the blue oceans and clouds below. So, he cut it into small puzzle pieces, then gave them to the boy as a puzzle to put back together.

> I'm afraid we have gotten away with doing the least He has asked, instead of the most He has asked.

In just a few minutes the boy was back and wanted to show his dad that he had put the puzzle together. Now, the dad thought he may have a genius on his hands, because he had cut it in lots of really small pieces and they were mostly blue oceans and clouds.

The dad asked the boy how he did it so quickly.

The boy had taped it together, so he turned it over and said, "Dad it was easy! On the other side is a picture of a man. I put the man together, and the world came together."

It is the same with us. Are you allowing God to put you back together?

FOUR

The Disciple-Maker Explained

Back in 2004 I got to be part of Dream Builders Network in Orlando, Florida. Kennan Burch, a great friend of mine, had a dream of helping men to find and live their dreams. Not dreams they drum up from the fleshly desires of society, but dreams God gave them. "For we are his workmanship, created in Christ Jesus for good works, which God prepared beforehand, that we should walk in them" (Eph. 2:10). When we started, we had a momentous stadium event. I got to be part of the launch video in which a bunch of dream-builders stated their dream. In my time on the video I said, "I want to help churches come alive and answer the question, 'What do you think Jesus meant when He said Go?'" I thought then what I think now: Jesus meant GO! and make disciples. "Go," a verb, not a noun.

In the New Testament the word Christian is used three times. The words for believer, believes, believing, belief, and believe are used about 177 times. They are interchangeable with our word faith, a verb and noun contained in the same Greek word.

However, the shocker is this. The words disciple, disciples, discipled, and discipling are used 268 times. Of those times, 265 are nouns and three are verbs. Of the three verbs, two are passive, and one is an imperative verb. Only one time in the entire New Testament this word is used as an imperative verb. Let that sink in. Only one time. And that single time the word disciple is used as an imperative verb is when Jesus used it in Matthew 28:19. One time!

Jesus coined a term.

Jesus said, go, and as you are going, make disciples! He was the only one to use the word disciple as an imperative verb. I may be the only one other than English teachers who sees this as amazing.

The only time in the entire Bible!!! It is never before or after used as a verb. One time. Has that

Jesus coined a term. fact sunk in yet? Jesus meant, go do what I showed you. What He had shown his disciples was not a classroom or worship center setting a few hours a week where he engaged just their minds or emotions, and only for a few hours. His was a lifestyle of loving people, all people, as He went about in life.

Again, I'm not saying worship and Sunday School are bad. But this is too important, and too vital to miss. His disciples followed Him for three years. Day in and day out. Jesus taught them by showing them what it was like to love people and each other, as they went. To engage deeply with them. To intentionally invest in them. Regardless of who they were, where they came from, when He met them, or what type of person they were. Regardless of the time of day. Regardless of where He was. Regardless of where they were. He taught His followers by words and by daily actions and by actually loving them personally as He showed them how to love others. If the *message* of our Lord is important, the *method* of our Lord is of equal importance. I don't know who said that first, but they were right.

Is it possible for us to do this relational work here in the West? I believe it is. But we must realize it will take time. It will be messy. Many will misunderstand us. When we follow Jesus beyond the glass, we will upset those who want to remain behind the glass. Our movement will say to them, "you may need to change too." And they don't want to. Their aquariums are just fine. They are comfortable. A comfort zone is just that … comfortable. When we start to change things behind the glass of religious trappings, we will also upset the status quo of those behind the glass. Your "changing and moving" will create angst for those still behind the glass. These folks sound a little like Pharisees. I know, I felt like one at times. And Jesus coaxed me out. So, I now need to be patient with those who do not understand or like it. We need to be as loving and kind as Jesus was with Nicodemus. It was messy for Nicodemus even to meet with Jesus. It was beyond his glass. I think that is why he met Jesus at night.

There are way too many Christians sitting in church buildings throughout our land every week who think their job is done when they leave the premises or the Zoom meeting. Duty, obligation, and processes/programs have ruled the days of the past. But there are, I believe, even more folks sitting and hoping that there is something more for them than sitting in rows. They can no longer just sit there and mentally engage with a sermon, no matter how good it is. It is imperative that purposefully loving our neighbors, and anyone we meet, is what we are to be about if we are to follow the method of Jesus. Gathering in groups beyond our walls to do this, and seeing others grow in their abilities to do this, is imperative. Multiplying disciple-makers must become a new norm. I hope you think this too. You are up to the task, you know. Because the best disciple-maker ever lives inside you. And He is not done discipling you.

Disciple-making is a relational lifestyle, not a timeslot.

Here we will not start with the church organization or Sundays. We will not start with process or procedures. We will not start in the classroom or the worship time. We will start with relationships. With the Trinity, and with others.

In case your mind suggests that I am saying the mind is not important, I am not. You are reading and

Disciple-making is a relational lifestyle, not a timeslot.

processing right now. You have just thought through words of scripture which our Great Father saw fit for our Lord to say. He then inspired men to write it all down, so we could know Him deeply, not simply textually. The Spirit has been at work in your mind concerning the fact that the word disciple is only used once as an imperative verb. And that was by Jesus. You might have wondered, "Why did I not know that?" You may have thought, "What does that mean for me?" It is a fact that your mind is already engaged, and your heart has to do something with that fact. Jesus imperatively said "go make disciples." That is a relational heart command, not just a factual expectation. But doing that can get you in trouble.

In John 5:15-18 we see the Jews wanting to kill Jesus. And Jesus Himself then addressed them in 39-40 as He said, "You search the Scriptures because you think that in them you have eternal life; and it is they that bear witness about me, yet you refuse to come to me that you may have life." They were looking to the text alone and missed the One who wrote it.

Eternal life Himself was standing right there talking to them.

They missed Him. Again, this written text, this Bible we now have, is the only book ever written in the history of books—the only one EVER written—which, every time you pick it up to read it, you can talk to the Author. Do you? I realize I'm repeating what I have said. It is that important.

Too much of the time I know I have read it with the intent of *learning about God,* instead of *getting to know God.* I still struggle with this. I read for content, not relational intent. Yet it is His relational intent that I should be looking for. It is He Himself revealing Himself and His ways to me. At times, I still miss Him. He is not a text; He is a person. A Person to know with my heart and my mind. And He loves me! He loves you!

Eternal life Himself was standing right there talking to them.

God inspired the minds and the hearts of the writers of the biblical text. Jesus was the maker of everything, so, in essence, Jesus created the Bible. But, while on earth, He wrote nothing. He could have showed up to read that passage from Isaiah, and then that week said something like this to His disciples. "Now, I am going to write some new commandments for y'all to follow. It will take me all week, but I can get this "New Covenant" written by Friday. Then, I am going to die, and come back to life in three days, give you the Spirit to guide you and to live within you, and I will go back to Heaven and get things ready."

He could have said that. But He didn't. Yes, He was crucified and came back to life, securing salvation for those who believe. He did give us the Holy Spirit to guide us after that. But He wrote nothing. Nothing. He chose to take twelve men on a three-year relational journey where He showed them how to love God and love others—up close and very personal.

If our Lord took three years showing twelve men how it's done, we are not going to get trained in a weekend seminar.

I hope we all become followers, disciples, and disciple-makers. So, please stop what you are doing just long enough to ask yourself some deep relational questions. Honestly attempt to process your answers with other believers and treat the answers as precious and healing. You can move further toward being a disciple who is a disciple-maker—one who follows Jesus well, and helps others follow Jesus well … all week. Will you lay down your life to see Him come to life?

My hope is that you will intentionally develop relationships as you go.

And as you "go to church," you can help breathe some life into dying processes, programs and meetings.

That is my hope.

FIBONACCI, FRACTAL GROWTH, AND GOD'S REPRODUCING IDEAS.

God creates, then re-creates from what He created. He told Adam and Eve to multiply. Also, every animal, every tree, plant, fish, everything has come from what came before. Everything found in nature is re-produced from what came before. What if God intends His nature and His character to be re-produced in us in the same way? What if in the spiritual world, a relationship with Him follows that same pattern of re-production. We know that we are loved by Him, and therefore we are to go love others with His love. John 13:34-35 says, "A new commandment I give to you, that you love one another: just as I have loved you, you also are to love one another. By this all people will know that you are my disciples, if you have love for one another." With the same love He has for us, we are to love others. We then tell them where that love came from, Him. Then they go and do the same, repeating that with others. His character, His love, would then be reproduced, time and time again. It is that simple. And we have gummed it up with too many processes and too much about the mind and not enough about the heart of God and relationships. Again, don't get me wrong, the mind is important. But without love from the heart, we sound like clanging cymbals.

> And as you "go to church," you can help breathe some life into dying processes, programs and meetings.

God's whole point was this: that you come to know Him through Christ ... gain access to His character ... that character lives and grows in you ... and then, through the Spirit, that character helps others see Him in you ... then they repeat the relational process. In Galatians 2:20 Paul wrote, "I have been crucified with Christ. It is no longer I who live, but Christ who lives in me. And the life I now live in the flesh I live by faith in the Son of God, who loved me and gave himself for me." What Christ did for Paul, in the past, was changing his present, so that he could live for Him in the future. Christ set Paul free, and he then helped set others free.

It is a relational process that moves forward, creating ahead of it what has been before it.

Now think of it this way. God said His divine attributes can be found in nature. "For his invisible attributes, namely, his eternal power and divine nature, have been clearly perceived, ever since the creation of the world, in the things that have been made" (Rom. 1:20). The fact that He exists is evident in the things that have been made. His attributes can be seen. He has set in motion a reproducing earth. What if He has been trying to reinforce that premise for us to spiritually reproduce, to multiply? By showing His nature in earthly nature, He is consistent. He changes us, and then we help someone change by showing His attributes to them. Again, what if it was that simple? But we try to box it up, to multiply it by our methods, and contain it— all the while He is trying to tell us to use His methods and release it. Setting captives free was what Jesus was about ... not sticking caught fish in an aquarium. Those free fish set other captives free. That is our main spiritual purpose right in the middle of all our lives, families, and jobs. Remember Isaiah 61:1 and Luke 4:18. He came to set captives free.

It is a relational process that moves forward, creating ahead of it what has been before it.

Spiritually, that which is the same has built on what came before. There was a beginning. And growth came from that beginning. Jesus is our beginning. He was, and is, and is to come. There was that which existed before the beginning of beginning. Hold on. I'm not getting metaphysical here or going down a rabbit hole. God's character and attributes have existed in Him, as Him, in forever past. Getting to know Him and then imparting that spiritual relational knowledge through relationships to others, building His kingdom (not ours), is His desire. This process could go on and on and on and on and on and on. I think this is a "spiritual Fibonacci sequence" or "fractal spirituality." What (Who) has always existed as the great "I Am." And He always has been. He creates. Then re-creates. Then re-creates. His nature of building on what came before is evident. And He predates the material universe. So, the fact that we are related to the "Great I Am," means we are reproducing what came before time. "I Am" wrote down what He wanted us to know about Him and His nature as it relates to humans and redemption. Even I have a hard time following all that. But I think it is true. Because He is true.

> These Fibonacci numbers are statistical and spatial. But we are spiritual and relational.

The Italian mathematician Leonardo of Pisa, later known as Fibonacci, discovered a mathematical sequence. In his 1202 book *Liber Abaci*, Fibonacci introduced the sequence to Western European mathematics, although the sequence had been described earlier in Indian Mathematics.

The Fibonacci sequence is expressed in a mathematical statistical formula. From the Oxford dictionary: "each part of which has the same statistical character as the whole."

These Fibonacci numbers are statistical and spatial. But we are spiritual and relational.

Fractals and the Fibonacci sequence are found perfectly and almost flawless in so many areas of creation. In all the parts of creation which have no soul—pinecones, daisies, sea shells, galaxies, sunflower pistils, leaves, hurricanes, rose petals. They follow a spiral sequence. But fallen man does not follow the spiritual reproductive sequence God intended. It is a broken sequence. The image does not show perfectly all the time. And many times not at all. The sequence has been broken since we got here. We do not represent His character well. Too much of the time we represent the character of our birth father, Satan. Read John chapter eight. We are born with him as our spiritual father. But God had a plan.

What God started, He has continued. And will continue. "And I am sure of this, that he who began a good work in you will bring it to completion at the day of Jesus Christ" (Phil. 1:6). The enemy disrupted the perfect order God had created. The disruption started with the rebellion of Satan and one third of the angels, and then the fall of mankind. The perfect reproduction has flaws from birth. Physical flaws. Spiritual flaws. Emotional flaws. Soul-deep flaws. We are born dead in our trespasses and sins. But God has a plan to restore, to redeem, to draw people to Himself. All of nature cries out that He exists, and nature reproduces its own kind, as God said in Genesis. His divine nature is perfect. But it is represented imperfectly in the world we see because it is fallen. Yet even in the midst of the earth's fallen state, His nature and His attributes are visible in things that have been made.

Spiritual things cannot be measured well but are increasingly visible as they grow.

Spiritual reproduction, or disciple-making, is not perfect or algorithmic in nature. It is relational in nature. Therefore, it is messy. It does not perfectly follow a Fibonacci sequence. We are to re-produce that which has come before us, and which has always been. I know. This sounds a bit like Yoda or Confucius. Yet we are being conformed into His image. In Romans 8:29 God says, "For those whom he foreknew he also predestined to be conformed to the image of his Son, in order that he might be the firstborn among many brothers." If you are being conformed to the image of Christ, an image that has always existed, His image should be increasingly evident in your life.

I'm not trying to mystify or complicate. Since God is the creator, He gets to define the spiritually relational re-creative system. So why not start with His design, and talking to Him who created all things? The author of the bestseller of all time, the Bible. He redeems. He sanctifies. He glorifies. He has a spiritual growth order in His heart and mind for us and who we are to be. As mankind, we are to assist in that growth—which is disciple-making. A "spiritually relational" Fibonacci growth sequence. Again, it is not mathematical growth, it is spiritually relational growth.

Again, you cannot fish in an aquarium.

Spiritual things cannot be measured well but are increasingly visible as they grow.

Disciple-making is the overarching intent of everything God desires. It is the main thing Christ asked us to do: spiritually relational reproduction. For years I have had the following definitions running in the background of my mind:

- *A disciple is a believer who lovingly and increasingly seeks the face of the Father, exhibits the character of the Son and follows the lead of the Spirit, all to the glory of God in the church and in the world.*
- *A disciple-maker is someone who helps that happen in the life of someone else.*

This requires ongoing intentional relationships with the Trinity. How they change us, and how we help others do the same. Follow Jesus, and He will make us fishers of men. He already had it simplified in Matthew 4:19. He will make you a fisher of men. Jesus connects us to His Father, and then they connect us to His Spirit, and then us to others … to repeat. Ongoing relationships with the Trinity will take you beyond your bounds, beyond your glass. Beyond where you are.

Again, you cannot fish in an aquarium.

It is nutty to try to catch what has already been caught. But what has been caught needs to be released. You can help those near you who know Christ to become "fishers of men," but you should not catch more and put them in your aquarium. That defeats the purpose. If in your mind, the room/house your small group meets in is all there is, then when it is full, you have to quit reaching out to others. I have had small groups tell me they don't want to move to another room, or another house, or spin off another group because they were full, and happy with what they had. They had decided to die in their aquarium.

> I don't want to put any new fish alongside those who seem to want to float upside down.

I don't want to put any new fish alongside those who seem to want to float upside down.

You don't want to re-produce death. You want to reproduce life. God's Fibonacci sequence is that we reproduce that which came before. That means we need more space in front of us to start new discipleship relationships which help others form new groups, which in time, will do the same. All with the same relationships to the Trinity. E.V. Hill, a great pastor from the last century, told me one evening as we had supper together, "Never give your babies away." He explained that we should make certain that any new people or new believers in our church, our lives, or our groups … we should make certain that they are around people who will nurture them and help them to become fishers of men. Again, the process of re-producing that which came before.

FIVE

The Three Questions

Before we launch into how the three questions function, we have to start with you and the Trinity. How the three Persons of the Trinity are the Trinity, and relate to us. We start with prayer about ourselves concerning these three questions to all three Persons of the Trinity. If we don't, we might turn them into another program. The three questions help us know where we are and where others are spiritually. They help us move forward in following Him. They will help others do the same. But you must start with you. If you treat these as some church growth model, you will fall flat.

I know you are probably thinking, really, three questions … that's it … three simple questions will change things? Yep, they will. The difference here is that the three questions are all three looking Him straight in the eye. Facing directly at Him—all three of Him. All three questions focus on all three of Him and His activity in our hearts, and our minds, and our whole lives.

One of the hardest things to realize about this relational Trinity is this: if you talk to any one of the Trinity, the other two hear and know. Always.

They all love you and want to see you become the you They

see already. God the Father is not only the sovereign Holy Father—He wants to be your Abba Father. Jesus is not only Savior and Lord—He also wants you to grow into His likeness. The Spirit is not only your comforter and constant companion—He also is to be your guide throughout your whole life.

I dare you to ask all three of these questions and look to Him for answers. He is God and He is listening. Are you focusing on Him, or on your nice little setup in your aquarium? If you don't want positive change in your life, do not ask these questions. But if you do, positive change will be great, and as I've said, possibly messy. These "Three Relational Questions" will help you determine how you are doing as a follower of Him. They help me daily.

> **One of the hardest things to realize about this relational Trinity is this: if you talk to any one of the Trinity, the other two hear and know. Always.**

Father, how can I know and love You better?

Jesus, what needs to change so I look more like You?

Spirit, who are You leading me to invest in?

I ask these questions to Him, Them, in the morning as soon as I get up. Then I continue to ask them as I go about my day. My day needs to be His day. As followers, we are always related to all three of the Trinity. Why not access those relationships to the fullest? When we get to the "Six Relational Habits," they will help us define ways to keep the questions moving forward. They will help us determine how we move from where we are and show us areas for potential relational change, and how to develop it. These are not formulas. They are relational intents of life and character change we are to live by. But for now, focus on three questions.

What follows is not a perfect pattern, but a relational template starting with three questions. It is not a process to follow as a pattern, as though a pattern or process will work. These relational questions will help you and those you lead/disciple to be able to connect to the three Persons of the Trinity in deepening ways, and then move forward toward others, behind the glass and beyond the glass. These questions happen in concert, and all the time. The Trinity is never apart.

WAYS OF ASKING THEM

You must start with you, and how you love God. Why not just start asking Him?

The three questions I ask Him in prayer:

Father, how can I know and love You better?
Jesus, what needs to change so I look more like You?
Spirit, who are You leading me to invest in?

These three work in concert, as does the Trinity. You, as a disciple, are to get as relationally close as you can to Them, as well as Their work in Their kingdom.

- **Father, how can I know and love You better?**
  - » He looks at your heart. Are you looking at His heart?
  - » Renew your mind and your heart so you know Him and how deeply He loves you.
  - » The more you face Him and stare at Him, the more you will reflect His image.

- **Jesus, what needs to change so I look more like You?**
  - » Do you see Him for who He truly is, knowing your character can change because of Him?

» He loves you enough to not allow you to stay the same and wants your character to change so you look like Him.

» If you are being conformed to the image of Christ, His image should be increasingly evident in your life. His character should be increasing in your life, which would be a change from your birth character.

- **Spirit, who are You leading me to invest in?**
    » Do you really see and love people? He is guiding/sending you to love them.

    » Do you trust Him enough to allow Him to decide who, and when, and how?

    » Do you really see Him as your guide, and not just the One who comforts you and guarantees your entrance into Heaven?

The three questions I ask myself—as I read/study His Word:

There are so many ways to read, study, and apply scripture. Asking three relational questions of what He has written will help you to find Him, His ways, how He and people related well (or didn't) and how those people affected others ... for good and for bad.

- **What do I see about God here?**
    » Look for Him—How could I know Him better?

- **What character traits (good or bad) do the main people in the text exhibit?**
    » Look for change—How can I exhibit the good traits and avoid the bad ones?

- **How are others in the text affected by the traits of the main characters?**
  - » Look for how people affect others. How are the others in my life affected by me?
  - » Who is positively investing in whom on purpose?
  - » Who is helping others move forward spiritually?
  - » Who is hindering others from finding Him?

The three questions I ask myself:

- **How do I know and love my Father better?**
- **How am I changing so I look more like Jesus?**
- **How am I doing with those the Spirit is leading me to invest in?**

The three questions I ask others:

I do not actually ask these each time groups meet or with a person. But it would not be a bad idea to get in the habit to keep the topic and intent fresh and focused. You don't want to become rote, pharisaical, or legalistic. But for me, they help point meetings and groups in an intentionally relational spiritual direction. For groups to gain the spiritual depth we want, these have to be a constant reminder.

- **How do you know and love our Father better since the last time we met?**
- **What needs to change for you to look more like Jesus?**
- **Who is the Spirit leading you to invest in?**

These questions are imperative to your spiritual growth and the change and development of your soul.

It is good if we can regularly ask these to Him—of the biblical text as we read what He wrote—to ourselves as we contemplate where we are—and to others as we help disciple them to do the same. A simple chart can remind us to always seek Him, change in ourselves, and others.

TO HIM	AS WE STUDY
TO OURSELVES	TO OTHERS

God has arranged the scriptures He wrote so that they cover what He wants you to know and to do as you love Him, yourself, and others. In Matthew 28:19-20, the Great Commission, He says that we are to baptize in the name of the Father and of the Son and of the Holy Spirit. All three of the Trinity are mentioned. Why? It has to do with more than water immersion and it has to do with their name.

First, *the water*. When water baptism is mentioned, the Greek word *baptidzo* is used. It is the same one used throughout the New Testament. It also is used to mean immersed. In Acts 16:14, if Lydia were dying purple goods, she would have immersed them in purple dye to get the linen cloth, or whatever cloth she was dying, to become more purple. Its identity would be changed. It even says she was a "seller of purple goods" (Acts 16:14). God does not say she sold aprons, blouses, skirts, backpacks, etc. Everything she sold was now defined by what it had been immersed in. In the same way, we are to be defined by "who" we are immersed in. The more immersed we are, the more "purple" we are, the more we look like Him.

Second, *the name*. We are not just immersed in Him; we now carry His name. Growing up I borrowed my dad's tools to work on my car. They were dad's tools because he owned them. He bought them. Many of them had his initials engraved on them.

In *Toy Story*, Woody has Andy's name on the sole of his boot. We have God's name engraved on our soul. We should know that, and act like we have taken His name. I remember a friend whose dad would always say as he left the house to go somewhere, "Remember who you are!" He knew he carried the same last name as his dad. He was representing that family everywhere he went. We represent our God everywhere we go. So, the three questions help to remind us we are always connected to the Trinity.

> God is telling us that we should be consistently "being immersed" in who He is. Then being re-defined by who He is. And then letting others know who He is. All at the same time.

We always carry Their name. But how well are we carrying those names? Do we remember whose we are?

God is telling us that we should be consistently "being immersed" in who He is. Then being re-defined by who He is. And then letting others know who He is. All at the same time.

Remembering that always will keep us close to Him. None of the three of Them are caught off guard when you are praying. None of the three are surprised when you think something stupid. None of Them are clueless as to what you are dealing with in your soul. So ask these questions of the Trinity first, before you go out and think these three questions are only some form of discipleship model. They must start with you and your relationship to the Trinity. They will disciple you as you go.

If you are not drawing near to God, if you are not seeking the change you need in your own character by asking Jesus, and if you are not asking the Spirit whom to invest in … you are missing the whole point of a relational Trinity.

DISCIPLINES. FRUIT. GIFTS.

Lining up with these three questions are *spiritual disciplines, spiritual fruit, and spiritual gifts.* This could really be a whole other book. Disciplines, fruit, and gifts—are all from Them and for Them. Their desire is that you are disciplined enough to continually get to know Them as They truly are. As you develop these relationships with Them, you can't help but notice how you are "not" like Them … and you may bear little or no fruit. But as you do bear fruit, you take that fruit to wherever your gifts are needed for your church and for the life you live.

Spiritual disciplines help you answer question one. Spiritual disciplines lead us to a deepening relationship with God first, to "discipline yourself for the purpose of godliness" (1 Tim. 4:7 NASB). In his book *Spiritual Disciplines for the Christian Life*, Donald Whitney says, "There is an invitation to all Christians to enjoy God and the things of God through the Spiritual Disciplines."[8] They start with Him, but do not end with Him. Disciplines are not about being disciplined, but are about drawing close to Him.

Spiritual fruit is a result of question two. Spiritual fruit is the expected result of that deep abiding relationship with God, and how you change in Christ. Fruit is what God desires to see all of us produce because of our relationship with Him. These fruits are not based on whether your personality is introverted or extroverted but are for all of us as evidence that we are connected to Him. John records Jesus saying this, "If you abide in me, and my words abide in you, ask whatever you wish, and it will be done for you. By this my Father is glorified, that you bear much fruit and so prove to be my disciples" (John 15:7-8). We tend

---

[8]Donald Whitney, *Spiritual Disciplines of the Christian Life* (Colorado Springs: NavPress, 1991, 2014), 19.

to see this passage as about getting what we want. But John is talking about abiding in Christ. John recorded what Christ said. The whole first half of chapter fifteen in John's gospel is about becoming like Christ, not about stuff. The more we become like Christ because we abide in Him and His Word, the more we will ask for what He wants in our lives. But more importantly, we will look like Him in the fruit of our character.

Spiritual gifts are how question three moves you along in your life. Spiritual gifts, given to each of us, make us a distinct part of the body in how we serve and help the body to grow. These are all different for each person. We are unique. These gifts also help define uniquely what jobs or type of work we do. We all go to different places during the week and can serve in different areas in the church. Our gifting helps define where and what we do even in our vocation. As we go and use our gifts, the fruit of a relationship with Him should be evident.

Disciplines connect us to Him, so we see fruit grow, and gifts are where we show the fruit and how we help the body function. These three—disciplines/fruit/gifts—work in concert, not alone. Just as the Trinity works together, our disciplines, fruit, and gifts are a part of our whole being growing us into the likeness of Christ. The six habits reinforce these as we ask the three questions. These relational questions must be asked *intentionally* and *relationally*. Only then will they help the life of Christ to be *reproduced* in you and others, helping all to mature through the stages of Christian growth.

As you ask the three questions of yourself and others, you can't help but live beyond the glass. You will find yourself in areas of spiritual life with Him you didn't even know existed. The amazing part of His grace is that He is the One who is guiding you in the answers to the questions. It is not you coming up with the answers. The more closely I have listened over the years, the more I have found myself beyond the glass without even realizing it. Developing disciplines and fruit and gifts positions me to be more of use to Him out there. They will help you also to move beyond the glass. It is like a timid child who has been coaxed from behind the furniture and onto the back porch. They hear the "mmmmmm" sounds of a trusted adult as they eat an ice cream cone outside. The child forgets that they were scared. Before you know it, they are sitting next to you, eating ice cream, and talking up a storm. We know what good things we have for our children ... and our heavenly Father knows what good things He has for us.

HOW THE 3 QUESTIONS RELATE TO THE 6 RELATIONAL HABITS

The three questions and six habits are to be developed all the time, everywhere. Seeing that they are all based on the Trinity, if you can remember God the Father, Son and Holy Spirit, you can remember the questions. The six relational habits develop the relationships as they fulfill the questions. An element of each can be in every encounter and every part of your day.

Remember, disciple-making is a lifestyle, not just a time slot or a place. However, to the degree that you or your group only focus on one aspect, one question or one habit, you will not develop in all areas of your spiritual life. It is good to focus on each one to grow, but don't only focus on one. To the degree you are allowing Him to work with you in all the habits, you are moving forward. No one ever finishes. No one is ever perfect except in God's eyes. Everyone has the opportunity to grow/ change in all areas. Some changes in your life may indicate you are growing in one area, and yet another may indicate you need to mature in another area. Be patient. He loves you insatiably and is working on you.

These habits are basically core values with expectations as part of them. Core values tend to be static statements. The habits are directly connected to your relationships with the Trinity, your relationships with each other as followers of Christ, and your relationships with those who do not know Christ (or have no group/church they can follow Christ with). They are practical, intentional ways of carrying out the great commandment and the great commission within daily relationships in your community. They will accomplish multiplying the life of Christ in your life and the lives of others. It is hard to pragmatize these relational intentions. But, please come up with your own words or phrases that fit where God is leading you or your church. Make these relationships yours and remember, it is not your church. It is His church. The following chart shows how the three questions, the disciplines-fruit-gifts, and the six habits relate to one another.

THREE QUESTIONS	SPIRITUAL GROWTH	SIX HABITS
Father, how can I know and love You better?	Spiritual disciplines	· Finding the Person of God · Immersing in Him
Jesus, what needs to change so I look more like You?	Spiritual fruit	· Getting Out Lets Others In · Cultivating Community
Spirit, who are You leading me to invest in?	Spiritual gifts	· Serving Our Circle and Beyond · Going Outside

Though these are ordered and numbered, they are not intended to be linear. Don't do the first habit, and then after a year when you think you've got it down, start the second habit. Think about all of these at the same time. You are probably saying, "I can't think of six habits and three questions. It's overwhelming." Those are normal feelings. But realize that once you see how tightly tied together they are, you will see that you can. But even though they are not linear, you must start with God. To start with anything but God, is to miss everything else.

> Question One and Habit One start with our Father and what He has written. If you ever feel like you are getting off track, go back to One. He will lovingly order the next steps.

Question One and Habit One start with our Father and what He has written. If you ever feel like you are getting off track, go back to One. He will lovingly order the next steps.

The Trinity has existed forever. Our decisions to think about Them and how we actually relate to Them every minute of every day may be new. It is a new habit to me. It is not how I have been much of my past life. But it is now how I try to live all day every day. The six habits are also not new. You have probably seen these disciplines in various forms in many other places. However, here they are specifically attached as relational expectations to each Person of the Trinity. They are not just a duty or obligation. They are relational habits by which we position ourselves to receive grace from God, which is desperately needed to be a part of our life all day. In his book *Habits of Grace*, David Mathis says, "'the means of grace,' and the practice (habits) that ready us to go on receiving God's grace in our lives, this much must be clear from the outset: The grace of God is gloriously beyond our skill and technique. The means of grace are not about earning God's favor, twisting His arm, or controlling His blessing, but readying ourselves for consistent saturation in the roll of His tides."[9]

The following is a short explanation of the habits that go with the three questions. They will be explained in much more detail later.

THE 3 RELATIONAL QUESTIONS & 6 SPIRITUAL RELATIONAL HABITS:

All six of these habits are participial phrases. They are meant to happen all the time, as you are going. There are two habits for each of the three questions, which blends them all together. Remember the engine. Three fluids, six cylinders, all working in concert. But you are required to get in the car and start the engine. Let's look at a short paragraph about each one before we go more deeply. If I knew you, I would be asking you each of these questions or looking to see how they are playing out in your life:

Question 1—How do you know and love our Father better since the last time we met?

Habit 1—Finding the Person of God—Life works better when you consistently read and study the written Word with the desire of drawing near to God, knowing Him and His ways more intimately daily. Getting to know the author and speaking with Him and *worshiping* Him individually and corporately. More than just reading His text. John 5:39-40, 2 Tim. 3:16-17, Psa. 119:11, Ex. 33:7-10, Deut. 6:4-9, Luke 24:27, 44-45, Heb. 4:12-13.

Habit 2—Immersing in Him—To develop and experi-

---

[9]David Mathis, *Habits of Grace* (Wheaton: Crossway, 2016), 21.

ence a deeper relationship with the living Word, Jesus Christ, we must learn to abide in Him. Drawing near to the Living Word is relationally imperative. If you don't start with the Word, you are flying blind, or swimming blind.

Abiding is a direct response to engaging the Word. It means to connect with Him and experience Him through the *spiritual disciplines* of worship, studying His Word, prayer, journaling, fasting, etc. John 15:4-8, Matt. 4:10, Gal. 5:16-26, Eph. 6:10-18, Phil. 3:7-11.

Question 2—What character traits need to change for you to look more like Jesus?

Habit 3—Getting Out Lets Others In—Becoming transparent and vulnerable with one another about the areas of our lives in which we need to grow in the character of Christ is imperative. Our relational needs are important. Christ can meet them all. But we need each other for them to work. It involves the ability to confess the areas we struggle with, to then be able to disciple one another and to pray for one another without condemnation. To encourage one another in the work of maturing and growing *spiritual fruit* which comes because of abiding. Notice how the *one anothers* are vitally important to real relationships. Rom. 8:29, 2 Cor. 3:18, Jas. 5:16, 1 Thess. 5:11, Rom. 8:1, Heb. 3:12-13, 2 Tim. 2:2.

Habit 4—Cultivating Community—The more transparent we are, the more authentic our community/group becomes. The more intentionally we focus on deepening our relationship with Christ and then others, the more we relax and become family. Good family. We can help each other see the ways in which we can grow *spiritual fruit*. This involves spending consistent, quality time in relationships centered around God and His

Word, and the *spiritual fruit* He wants to develop in us. Call it fellowship if you want. But make certain it is not just about gathering and food. Gal. 5:22, John 13:34-35, Acts 2:42-47, Heb. 10:24-25, 1 Cor. 12:1-26, Eph. 4:11-16, 1 Cor. 13:13, Gal. 6:1-5.

Question 3—Who is the Spirit leading you to invest in?

Habit 5—Serving Our Circle and Beyond—People who are mature, and are maturing, are those who give of themselves and their possessions for the sake of others. Giving of ourselves is our spiritual service. Giving of our time, talent, and treasures is our privilege to help mature others to become disciple-makers themselves. Knowing our *spiritual gifts* will help us to know where we will shine the most. Not that God does not ask you to serve or give in areas you may not be gifted in. But don't neglect the gifts you do have. They are for the body of Christ and can be used for others to see who He is. Gifts are a reflection of Him. This is a team effort within each small group, and each church, and the church as a whole. We all help shepherd one another as we serve together and help each other do all of the above. 2 Tim. 2:2, Rom. 12:1-8, 1 Cor. 13, Matt. 20:25-28, Matt. 23:11, Mark 9:35, Luke 12:43, John 13:12.

Habit 6—Going Outside—Jesus left us with the life-mission of sharing the good news—evangelism—about Him with people who are far from God. Most of our waking hours are spent beyond the walls of a church building. Remember, we are the church. As disciples, we can consistently be encouraging one another to watch for those we can bless, invest in, and help draw near to Him … "as we go." All the while, being an example of someone who loves Jesus and follows Him. If we follow Him, we will follow Him outside the camp. "For the bodies of those animals whose blood is brought into the holy places by the high priest as a sacrifice for sin are burned outside the camp. So Jesus also suffered outside the gate in order to sanctify the people through his own blood. Therefore, let's go with him outside the camp and bear the reproach he endured" (Heb. 13:11-14). Outside the walls of our Jerusalem, our aquarium. We will help set the captives free. Matt. 28:19-20, Acts 1:8, 1 Pet. 3:15, Luke 14:23, Matt. 18:15-20.

SIX

A Deeper Look at the Six Habits

HABIT 1 - FINDING THE PERSON OF GOD.

When I was in my first semester of seminary, I actually took Systematic Theology. Yikes! I was green and didn't know the Bible well enough to talk about systematizing theology. But it was one of the last classes with a seat open. I thought I knew the Bible at least well enough to muddle through. On the first day of class the professor began by saying this, "In systematic theology, we must put God in a box." Well, I bristled at that. I was smart enough to know that was not possible. God did not want that of us. The professor went on to say, "We must do all we can to get our arms around God, who He is, to know Him, to define Him in our minds … our box … then we must allow Him to kick out the sides and dance on the lid." Now he had my attention. I learned in that class what it meant for me to discover God as I looked at what He had written from a systematic standpoint. The Author knows what He wants to say about Himself and His ways. Will I let Him? Will you? Habit One starts with Him. For without knowing Him personally, you are building your own box of theology. And you are god of that box. That is not going to work well at all.

Finding the Person of God seems like peering through murky water. But we can approach Him. Because He is approachable, and He is God. As we do approach Him, we need to realize two things to see Him more clearly:

One—We don't know Him completely.
Two—We believe some things about Him that are just not true.

There is a lot more of Him to get to know personally as the One who made us and planned a way to save us. We also need to discard our incorrect beliefs and replace them with true truth about Him—no matter how hard they are to un-learn.

Our knowledge is incomplete and somewhat wrong—that creates the murkiness. But we have a God who knows that, and cares. The water in our own fish tank and the water beyond the glass are both murky. Therefore, moving forward is tenuous at times. But not always. His desire is that you "Draw near to Him, and He will draw near to you" (Jas. 4:8). A deeper heart connection of relational knowledge with Him can and will remedy the two issues. God can clear things up. Getting to know Him solves everything. That can seem like an impossible statement right now. You or someone you love may have had COVID. You may have lost a loved one or a friend. You may have a different illness. You may be financially strapped. Life may seem unfair at the moment. Thoughts of suicide have come out of nowhere. Your heart may be breaking. It may feel like the enemy has demanded to "sift you," just as he demanded to have Peter so he could "sift him." But Jesus said to Peter, "but I have prayed for you that your faith may not fail" (Luke 22:32). Ask Him to pray that for you. If you are a follower of Jesus, He already has.

But to have Him say "but I have prayed for you," you must choose to open your arms to Him and be close enough to Him to hear Him say that. Peter was. You have that freedom to open your arms, open your heart. As followers, we must be looking intently at Him and listening closely to Him. As He said to Peter, He will say to us, "And when you have turned again, strengthen your brothers" (Luke 22:33). Peter knew Christ very personally. Peter was one of the first to get to know all three Persons of the Trinity. God is Christ, and Christ is God. The Spirit is God, too, and will guide us to know all three of Them—to know who They are. We cannot get to know Them simply by rote, ritual, or rigorous study. We have tried that. Those are not bad. They are just not enough. Again, remember that the Bible is the only book ever written that when you read it, you can talk to the Author. The relational connection we have with God through what Christ did on the cross allows us the freedom to be open and honest with Him about what we neither know nor understand—as well as what we do know but which may be false. We can trust Him. We can be open to new relational information and relational connection to a relational God, "from" our relational God. And not just with God our Father. But with Jesus our savior and the Holy Spirit our comforter and guide. Again, "You search the Scriptures because you think that in them you have eternal life; and it is they that bear witness about me, yet you refuse to come to me that you may have life" (John 5:39-40). Jesus said that to the purveyors of murky water ... the religious fog leaders of their time.

God loves us deeply and wants us to know Him deeply. He has given us all we need in His Word. We are the ones who miss it. We treat it as a textbook. We create religious fog, murkiness, for ourselves and others. Don't get me wrong. Don't stop reading, studying, and developing good habits. But they should drive you to Him, as a Person.

Personally, I have had a hard time doing this. Over the years I have gotten better. But when I am confronted with scripture which I know is true, and that scripture does

I tend to be His child more than He is my God.

not set well with a deeply held belief I have, I must talk to Him openly and freely and ask Him to guide me to understand Him. To get to know Him. Not just to know His truth, but more importantly to know Him as truth. I am fully His, but I do not treat Him as fully mine.

I tend to be His child more than He is my God.

He knew me completely before I knew the first thing about Him. He is always right and will always guide me to right thinking and right action, all based on right theology, all based on Him as a Person. The amazing fact is that He wants my heart to be focused toward Him. Again, there is that truth that He wants me to draw near to Him. And I love Him for that. Do you?

Life works better when you consistently read and study the written word with the plan of drawing near to the One who wrote it. Look at the text with the defined purpose of drawing near to God, knowing Him and His ways more each day. This will begin to break the glass of your prison. It is somewhat like realizing you have a hammer which can help you move forward through the glass. Getting to know the author and worshiping Him individually and corporately. If I want to get to know Him, the best way is to pick up what He wrote and read it, looking for

Him. I have to remind myself every time I look at His written Word, that He is there. Are you talking to the Author? Do you talk to Him every time you read it, every time you study it, every time you think about a particular passage? He deeply wants you to. He wants so much for you to know Him. I know you probably know this, but the following passages speak to this. These scriptures show that true life is about a personal relationship with the God of the universe. Read them again, looking for Him to speak to you about Himself. John 5:39-40, 2 Tim. 3:16-17, Psa. 119:11, Exod. 33:7-11, Deut. 6:4-9, Luke 24:27, 44-49, Heb. 4:12-13.

This is not just reading, studying, or a short devotional in the morning. Too much of the time we want a "kingdom without the king." That way, we get to be king. With some principles to make our lives a bit better, but no one telling us what to do. We engage with only the parts of the biblical text which fit what we want. We sometimes don't want the real King messing with our hearts. We take things out of context or we mix them with other religious ideas. That is syncretism. And it is never good. He knows what is best for us.

> **God is more knowable than any human person you can know.**

God is more knowable than any human person you can know.

Let that sink in. Our ability to know Him is skillfully hindered by the enemy and his distractions. It is hindered by our feelings and thoughts that there is no possibility to personally understand and know Him. We worry that our understanding of the text or our performance or explanation or how we will communicate the gospel will be judged. Instead of first and foremost approaching Him as a Person to be known, we look at Him as a text to be studied. We forget He is the Person who loves us, and we are to share Him with others. Nothing wrong with study. But study Him, the Person, not just the text. In this context, knowing with our mind does help a lot. But it starts with our heart for Him and His heart for us to know Him intimately as a Person. Go back and re-read the section on heart in chapter one. Drawing near to His heart is imperative!

As we get to know Him we are to teach/preach all the time. Sermons are not just for Sunday. Each and every one of us is an explainer of the gospel. We teach others about who God is by our actions, our attitudes, and the words we speak. We must seek to know Him deeply and be able to talk about Him easily as if we had all the stories of Him stored up and ready to explain at the drop of a hat. Without notes, without points, without the text. We don't need to just memorize scripture—we need to know Him. This does not come quickly. But knowing a Person along with some text is easier than just plain text. We need to know Him well enough to be ready to give an account for the hope that is within us. The hope is Him. Hope in a Person not a principle. How well do you know Him? Think about this—what if I asked you to tell me about a person you know well? What do you know about them? If I sat with you and said, tell me about them. You would start talking about the times you have had together. What they are like. How they act. How they think. How they react. What food they like. What they don't like. What types of books or movies they enjoy the most. You could go on and on. If I had taken all those notes down, all the stories, all the likes and dislikes—that is the beginning of the text about that person you know. God has done His writing first. You can engage with His written Word in such a way that you can tell the stories of scripture and point to all He is in all of them. You can talk about His likes, dislikes, desires, character traits. Yet all of that is a secondary reason. Your explanation is secondary. The primary reason for you to know Him is to know He loves you. He is a loving God toward you and wants you to know His love for you. You can know Him, see His character, His attributes, and Him as the Trinity. The fact is, that He is Jehovah Rapha, the God who heals you. This is why He said in the great commandment to love God and love others. He loves us. He wants us to love Him back, and then to love others.

Don't just memorize scripture only to win an argument. We always win, because He is always right. But in our talking with others, or our teachings, do they hear our words and know Him? Do they know He is love?

One of our Father's main intents in writing down all that He wanted us to know in the Bible is that we would know Him. Not just know about Him. But know Him. Have I said that too much? Is it sinking in that life is about relationships? First with Him? In Psalm 119:11 he has David (we assume) write that, "I have stored up your word in my heart, that I might not sin against you." He did not say mind. He said heart. Store it up. It is relational storage. Get to know Him. Because what you know of Him is all you can abide in. We are to abide in a person, not in the information about a person. Knowing Him with your heart, you can share that heart-knowledge with others so that they can know Him personally. Your mind alone, not connected to Him with your heart, and relying only on information and no deepening relationship with Him, can lead you down a path of legalism. Your heart alone, without true information about Him, can lead you to a shallow emotional relationship with Him where you are swayed by every wind of doctrine. But, connect your heart and your growing and genuine closeness to Him, along with your mind focused on Him as a Person. He has

said, "I will give you a future and a hope," that He will lead
your heart and your mind to Himself. He will guide you in the
paths of your life which He intends, which will be a part of the
great redemption narrative. In this way, others will see Him
and His ways in you as you walk this life. Notice the personal
pronouns in Psalm 119:11: "I have stored up your word in my
heart, that I might not sin against you."

I, your, my, you. David was speaking personally to God and
writing down what he said.

As we get to know Him, we learn to abide in Him.

There are days in which I am not as kind as I would like to
be. God will reveal this to me. I sometimes get envious. At times
I catch myself boasting and I get prideful
about something. At times I have dishon-
ored someone. But I'm not proud of that. I
have tended to be self-seeking, and in the
past I got angry pretty easily. At times I
have not been able to forget about a wrong
someone did to me. I have smiled when something did not go
someone's way. I have not had joy when truth was told. I have
not always protected others as I should and I have not always
trusted as I should. I want to be hopeful all the time, but at
times I do not persevere. Sometimes I just flat fail. I sin against
Him because I do not know Him well. The more "He'" as a
Person (not just text) is stored up in my heart, the more I see my
sin before it happens.

He has shown me all these over time. Person to person, His
Spirit telling my spirit. I ask a personal question to Him so I can
get to know Him better, not just for informational answers. "Father, can you show me how to know You and love You better?"
If you do this when you read what He has written, He will show

**As we get to know
Him, we learn to
abide in Him.**

you. Sometimes it is about how you treat Him or think of Him. Sometimes it will be about how you treat others whom He loves. I have a long way to go.

Go glance at "Traits'" in chapter seven. The left column is a short list of some opposites of love as in the fruit of the Spirit—traits which are not loving. They are the antitheses of the love listed in 1 Corinthians 13:4-7: "Love is patient and kind; love does not envy or boast; it is not arrogant or rude. It does not insist on its own way; it is not irritable or resentful; it does not rejoice at wrongdoing, but rejoices with the truth. Love bears all things, believes all things, hopes all things, endures all things."

In reading what He has written and trying to engage in a personal deepening relationship with Him, the One who wrote the text, He will show you who He is and how He works. In doing so, and realizing it, you will know Him better. You will also know yourself better. As you get to know our Father more deeply, you will begin to understand what it means to abide in Him. Since all habits are tied together, the shifts from one to another are more subtle than a simple mind shift. If you engage your mind to read and learn about Him with your mind, you engage your heart. If your heart is crying out to Him and you want to read and study and pray to get to know Him better, your mind will be guided. Our Father has a deep genuine desire for us to know Him. As you do, abiding in Him will increase. It will be more like immersing yourself in who He is.

HABIT 2—IMMERSING IN HIM.

As you get to know God more and more deeply, you will abide in Him more and He in you. The text about Him can't stay on the page; He must come alive in your heart. As your heart for Him does grow, you will become more and more transparent with Him, and then with others. A garment which is being dyed is immersed in water which has a different color than its own and takes on the characteristics of the water. Immersing yourself in Him, getting to know Him and His grace, is the point of it all…you abiding in Him. Nothing works well without that happening first. Jesus said, "You have seen me, you have seen the Father." In John 14:6-9 Jesus said,

> I am the way, and the truth, and the life. No one comes to the Father except through me. If you had known me, you would have known my Father also. From now on you do know him and have seen him." Philip said to him, "Lord, show us the Father, and it is enough for us." Jesus said to him, "Have I been with you so long, and you still do not know me, Philip? Whoever has seen me has seen the Father.

To develop and experience a deeper relationship with the living Word, Jesus Christ, it is essential that we learn to abide deeply in Him. Abiding is a direct response to getting to know the Person of God by engaging the Word of God. It means to connect with Him and experience Him through the spiritual disciplines of reading His Word, meditating, studying His Word, prayer, journaling, fasting, and other methods of finding the Person of God and immersing yourself in Him. But without your desire to connect on a relational personal heart level, these disciplines will seem dry as toast.

Sometimes we get to know Him through really tough circumstances. In Job 42:5 we read, "I had heard of you by the hearing of the ear, but now my eye sees you." Job got to know God better, but the circumstances are not what I would personally choose. Ron Dunn wrote a book, *When Heaven Is Silent*. We were in a few doctoral classes together, so I got to eat lunch with Ron many times. He was enduring difficult seasons. One son had committed suicide. The other was not doing well, and Ron's wife was also sick. Ron told me at lunch, "As I was praying one day, I said, 'God, next time you and Satan are talking, please don't bring up my name.'" And then he said that immediately the Spirit of God impressed him to say, "But if that is what You want to do to bring glory to Yourself, then so be it." At that moment, I knew I was sitting at the wrong lunch table. I was just not sure I could bring myself to say to the Spirit, "Whatever you need to lead me into, to do in my life that will bring glory to God, do it."

It was hard for me, getting to know God as more than a set of rules and obligations, and duties and attendance. I grew up thinking that life was a set of actions, steps to follow. Not wrong, I just didn't know Him well and the actions He wanted. And I sure did not want to tick Him off. Too much of my early years I spent doing what I wanted and trying to hide from Him for fear He would find me and lightning bolts would descend. After all, I probably deserved them for what I was doing. I had no clue how much He loved me. I knew He died on the cross. I knew that was love. But I knew nothing beyond that. I did not know He wanted to be an intimate ally living in me and willing to guide me all day every day. It has been a process for me to get to know Him as a Person and to be immersed in who He is.

Remember that we are baptized into Him. Is sho He is sinking into who you are? Is the fabric of your life being colored by Him? Remember Lydia and the purple cloth? This process has been, and still is, a staggering mystery to me. Even as I woke this morning, I still had that little question of Simeon, "How can these things be?" (John 3:9). The Spirit who is part of the Trinity, all of time, wants to guide me to do His work with Him. That I am working "with" Him as a part of the body, the bride of Christ, is inconceivable!

I have been helped in this process of abiding by three great books, and by men getting together to discuss them. Moving toward our Father to know Him as a Person is not a dry mental activity. It is a daily adventure in life of becoming more and more aware of His presence and work. He is always working even if I don't see it. Do I want to get in on it? If so, I must get to know Him. I tried for many years to work on His behalf, but without Him. Even though He was there and watching. It was as if I had a to do list and was off accomplishing it, planning to return to talk to Him tomorrow about it. All the while, He was there.

In *The Sacred Romance*, Brent Curtis and John Eldredge write about the incredible depth of closeness our Father desires to have with each one of us. They also talk about the wounds that the enemy wants to inflict so that none of us draw any closer to God, or others, than we currently are. Remember, the enemy wants to steal, kill, and destroy anything of God. "*The Sacred Romance* strikes a chord in us because more than in any other age, we have lost touch with our hearts. We have left that essential part of ourselves behind in the pursuit of efficiency, success, and even Christian service."[10] As I said, duty and obligation mostly won the day in my life. For me those two words were in the place where knowing the heart of a gracious Father should have been. And I didn't know it. As I have grown, and heartfelt

---

[10]Brent Curtis, John Eldredge, *The Sacred Romance* (Nashville: Thomas Nelson, 1997), https://www.amazon.com/Sacred-Romance-Drawing-Closer-Heart/dp/0785273425.

love has increased, I have realized it is what lasts forever. That realization continues today. And the enemy hates it.

The enemy inflicted a deep wound soon after John and Brent had published *The Sacred Romance*. In May of 1997 the two published that book. A year later, in May of 1998, at the inaugural "Wild at Heart" event, Brent Curtis died. It was a tragic and unexpected death. Brent fell eighty feet in a climbing accident at that event. John speaks of this in his book *The Journey of Desire*. It was written during that tough time after Brent's death. These books have helped me find my heart for God, but even more, His heart for me. All the while I have not disengaged my mind. My mind is fully aware of my heart's deep desire for Him. My heart and my mind now work much more in concert for me to be able to love Him as He has asked, with heart, soul, and mind.

The third book that affected me deeply was *Abba's Child* by Brennan Manning. Learning how intently God wants me to see Him as Abba Father was new to me. Viewing Him in this new way did not diminish my thoughts of Him as a great Father, high and lifted up. His greatness was not tarnished as He became approachable in my mind, then heart. In fact, I talk to Him much more now than I used to. Years ago I was not sure He had time for me. I did not think He was that interested in me. I figured He just loved me at a distance. Kind of like tolerating children who are around and are loud. For me it was like a warm blanket on a cold day to learn that He has joy when His children, including me, call His name. In Jeremiah 15:16, the prophet records this, "Your words were found, and I ate them, and your words became to me a joy and the delight of my heart, for I am called by your name, O Lord, God of hosts." The more we deeply know how He desires to call us by

His name, the more we can then deeply call Him by His name,
Abba Father.

HABIT 3—GETTING OUT LETS OTHERS IN.

It is imperative we become transparent with one another about
the areas of our lives in which we need to grow in the character
of Christ. It involves getting out there and letting others you
know, know you, and help you know Him as you deal with life's
struggles. Getting to know Christ and abiding in Him prepares
us for this. It involves the ability to confess the areas we wrestle
with to disciple one another and to pray for one another without condemnation. Romans 8:1: "There is
now no condemnation for those who are in
Christ Jesus." Never forget that!

> **Somebody has to start being open. It might as well start with you.**

You getting out of prison lets others in
on what freedom looks like. They need to
see it. Hear about it. We need to be transparent in our groups, and with our friends.
But many times being deeply transparent will take place only
in smaller groups of the same sex. By being transparent we
actually encourage one another in the work of maturing and
growing. This helps us grow spiritual fruit. I admit, this area
is where it gets messy. I struggle much concerning being open
about where I need to grow and where I need to change. The
places my mind takes my soul when it wants refuge. I begin to
succumb to the enemy's attempts to take me out. I really don't
like talking about my struggles and my failures. So I, like most
of you, walk around like nothing is wrong at all. I have it all together. The more we do that, the more others in our lives shirk
back into the corners of their lives, knowing in their hearts they
do not have it all together, while assuming our heart does.

Somebody has to start being open. It might as well start with you.

Each of us can, with courage, start with God and then move to a friend we already trust. See where it goes from there. The freedom you will experience is hard to explain. But when I do this, I know that my great God, my Abba Father who loves me, accepts me, and is working to change me into the image of His Son, will comfort me and guide me.

Sometimes being transparent starts with another person. Sometimes is starts with God. I would start with God. But many times, our scary or incorrect view of God limits our ability to talk ourselves into even approaching Him (as though He does not already know). Either way, transparency about what is going on in our heart and soul and mind is vitally important. You must be transparent— try starting with Him.

> That process of changing is to be talked about with others in such a way that they see Christ changing us.

I spent quite a few years knowing I created the shame Jesus had to wear. I was not sure what to do with that fact, or the shame. But I knew for sure that I did not want to face Him much because of that. I did not want to tell anyone else the things I had done in the past, or the thoughts I had that day which were certainly not godly. It took a long time for Romans 8:1 to sink in. Read it again slowly. "There is now no condemnation for those who are in Christ Jesus." Learning to live in Him means I had to learn how to live shame free and guilt free. I have to be able to admit who I am, what I was, what I have done, what I struggle with now, and how I grow in Him. It is a process.

That process of changing is to be talked about with others in such a way that they see Christ changing us.

This is painful at times. Change means we were not perfect.

In God's eyes yes, but in the eyes of others, no. We have faults. Our openness is not to glorify the flesh or glamorize what we have done. It is not to draw attention to ourselves. It is to draw attention to Him as the One who forgives and changes lives. I'm not sure where I heard the following, but I have embellished it a bit to make it my own as God has shown me who I am in Him.

Picture a courtroom. God is the judge, Satan is the prosecuting attorney, Jesus is the defendant's attorney, and you are the defendant. You stand as do all when the judge walks in. God sits in His seat. You all sit down. He reads the charge against you. And asks you directly, "How do you plead?" You say, "I plead guilty sir, I did that." God smiles with a wide, genuine, accepting smile, slams the gavel down, and says loudly, "Not guilty!"

The prosecuting attorney, Satan, stands and says, "Judge, are you serious? You just heard him confess he did it!!" To which God says, "Yes, I did hear him. I love it when My children confess what they did. In fact, he turned himself in. He heard My Spirit tell him that what he was doing was not according to what I wanted. He sinned. He knew it, then came to Me to confess it, and to be reminded of my forgiveness and love for Him. He is getting better and better, and stopping before he does some things that are not becoming of a child of Mine. We are helping him do that less and less. In fact, he looks more like My Son every day." Jesus smiles.

At that point Satan just stands there in disbelief. As you and Jesus begin to gather your things and walk out, Jesus notices you look a little down, distraught. He looks at you and says, "What's up? You look bothered!" You say, "Well I am. I still feel guilty and ashamed for what I did." Jesus says, "So you still have some guilt and shame—you still feel condemned?"

You say, "Yes." Then Jesus reminds you, "Remember what

I had Paul write, the fact that there is no condemnation for those who are in Me? And that I took all the shame and guilt for your sinful thoughts and actions? You do not bear the punishment for them though you did them. The guilt and the shame are gone. And now, it is my Spirit who points out these things to you so you will see you no longer need them. You can stop them. You have all you need in Me."

You say, "Yes I know all that, but I still have this." Then you show him a handful of shame and some guilt you have. He asks. "Where did you get that? That's not yours!" He then turns to look at Satan, who is about to leave and is trying hard not to make eye contact with Jesus, but he has to. Jesus says, "You are not leaving just yet."

Satan stops dead in his tracks. Jesus takes the guilt and shame from you and hands it to Satan. Jesus says to him, "Here, this is yours."

At this point I have to get into a piece of scripture which is contested a bit, about what happened when Christ died. In 1 Peter 3:18-20 God says, "For Christ also suffered once for sins, the righteous for the unrighteous, that he might bring us to God, being put to death in the flesh but made alive in the spirit, in which he went and proclaimed to the spirits in prison, because they formerly did not obey, when God's patience waited in the days of Noah." Jesus went to where those who died at the time of Noah were. That was not heaven, it was hell, or the holding bin, prison, depending on how you look at it. But it certainly was not heaven. They were still in prison. They never got out. They never took the opportunity to see God as their redeemer, as Noah and his family did. They went from prison on earth to prison in eternity. If you remember, in Genesis 6:11-13, God says, "Now the earth was corrupt in God's sight, and the earth was filled with violence. And God saw the earth, and behold, it was corrupt, for all flesh had corrupted their way on the earth. And God said to Noah, 'I have determined to make an end of all flesh, for the earth is filled with violence through them.'"

God said all flesh was corrupt and violent. Everyone but Noah and his family. It had gotten bad. Real bad. Anyway, Jesus went to where they were and proclaimed to those who died back at that point in time. Now, He did not say to them, "Anyone who doesn't like it here can come with Me." He proclaimed to them who He was. The One who took the penalty, the shame, the guilt, and the punishment for my sin. My personal belief is that He made a shame/guilt drop to Satan then and there—all the guilt and shame He took on the cross. He handed it all back over to Satan. It's all his, and that is where it belongs, with him.

If you belong to Christ, shame does not belong to you.

But the enemy will consistently try to hand some shame and guilt back to you.

Don't take it.

If you belong to Christ, shame does not belong to you.

The above story is not to convey to you that you just do as you like and God forgives. If you are truly His child, it breaks your heart when you sin. The Spirit's job is to convince you of it. It is not a free ticket—Jesus paid for that ticket. If you have that ticket, you have traded all the punishment for your sin and all the guilt and shame, for the righteousness of Christ. You are now not condemned. If you are not thankful for that, and do not currently relax in what He did for you, and you are still not concerned about tarnishing the Name who you now live for … you need to go back and re-think … did you really confess to Him and receive His forgiveness? Or did you just say some words in your mind but did not believe them in your heart? The enemy will trick you here also. He may try to get you to believe you really do not belong to Christ. That He has not covered your sin, and you are taking the punishment for it all. Ask God to show you where you are with Him. He will. I have had arguments about this. Some folks say that the shame is not over, and that is what motivates them to be better. I disagree. It is to be the love of Christ that motivates us, not shame. "For the love of Christ compels us, because we judge thus: that if One died for all, then all died; and He died for all, that those who live should live no longer for themselves, but for Him who died for them and rose again" (2 Cor. 5:14-15).

Letting others into your life is not easy. Our lives are messy at times. So are theirs. Some things are best said only in a men's group or ladies' group. It is not that you share about all the crap that is inside. It takes time and trust. And some people prove not to be trustworthy. They gossip. They need to be called out on that, but God forgives that too. But they must realize that gossip will end trust, and it can end your small group.

Sometimes we hide the real us and are not honest to God or others about our lives. Authenticity about your life, even the messy parts, is crucial to life as a disciple who follows Jesus. Brennan Manning, talking about what the imposter of himself says to himself, writes this, "Brennan, don't ever be your real self anymore because nobody likes you as you are. Invent a new self that everyone will admire, and nobody will know."[11] It is true. We wear masks to hide the real us. But that does not help us or anyone else get better.

It is not that we relish talking about our sin or our habits

---

[11]Brennan Manning, *Abba's Child* (Colorado Springs: Navpress, 1994, 2002), 25.

that we hide. But when we do, we need to talk about how great it is that Christ forgives us. How amazing it is that He gives us strength to push back against old habits. How utterly incredible we can walk with our heads held high knowing that He Himself walks with us and His Spirit lives in us, reminding us of who He is and who we are. We can help others know the close-knit relationship we have with our Lord. That is how authentic accountability happens.

Try some of the "one anothers" of scripture. There are about fifty specific one anothers. Chapter seven has most of them listed. Use James 5:16 in your small group: "Confess your sins to one another and pray for one another." When is the last time you divided up in groups of three and confessed your sins to one another? Now, I am not suggesting you do it that way. It is better done in a smaller group of just men or women. But, to the degree that you are not open with someone, another person or the guys (or gals) in the group, about the sin you are struggling with, you will not be transparent. And their prayers for you will be tepid because the prayers are not based on the truth of what you need. They will see the mask, not the real you.

All change from the life we once lived to the life we now live in Christ, requires change in character. In Galatians 2:19-20 Paul says, "I have been crucified with Christ. It is no longer I who live, but Christ who lives in me. And the life I now live in the flesh I live by faith in the Son of God, who loved me and gave himself for me." My life must change to be the life of Christ. As we abide in the vine, the vine produces good fruit in our lives. The fruit of the Spirit of Christ living in us.

NOTE: Gifts of the Spirit and Fruit of the Spirt are different. Think of them this way. Gifts are where and how you work/live. Fruit is what you exhibit/produce during your work/life.

Someone who is gifted at administration and someone who is gifted at teaching (gifts), should both learn to be patient as Christ is patient (fruit). It is number four on the list in Galatians 5:22. Both the administrator and the teacher should become peaceful as Christ is peaceful. Peace is number three on the Galatians list. All fruit should increase no matter your spiritual gifts.

We ask each other to help us be transformed—from our character to His character; from our actions to following His character and His actions; from our beliefs to His message and His method.

What you can do to help:

- Listen to people to know where they are.
- Help them move forward toward knowing Him.

What not to do:

- Ask someone to spill their guts in front of others when they are not ready.

Christ does not push. He allows. The rich young ruler is the one who opened up in front of Jesus and everyone. Jesus had to tell Him openly and lovingly what He needed to do. It was then on him. He chose to keep the same character trait he had, greed and selfishness. And he walked away sad.

What are the top character traits which must be exhibited for a disciple to know whether they are really in relationship with God? … Loving, humility, giving, serving? Love is the top. Everything else flows from it. God is love. We are to love others as ourselves. Living an un-loving life makes you a clanging cymbal. For every "fruit of the Spirit" there is an opposite fruit—bad fruit. Satan's brand of fruit is that of death. Since his plan is to steal, kill, and destroy, he goes after anything that looks like God. The Spiritual fruit we exhibit is of God. His Holy Spirit is the One who initiates it in our lives and gives us the power to live that way.

Our character must change. The fruit of the Spirit, attributes of Christ, actions of Christ, the "one anothers" all fit in the six relational habits. All of them together represent "Authentic Change." That change is attractive to people. Accountability in these areas grows your character and the characters of those around you. Your attitudes and actions which match the message and methods of Christ Jesus help grow your community—those you are around. Any name or attribute of God, Christ, the Holy Spirit that we as humans can emulate … we should emulate. (However, the three Greek words—omnipotent, omniscient, omnipresent = all powerful, all knowing, present everywhere, are obviously not for us.)

Maturing people exhibit sweet, maturing, spiritual fruit.

Think about Jehovah Rapha—the "God who Heals." As He heals us, we can help others see Him as a healing God. They'll see how His healing works in our lives, while it also helps to heal the bad emotions of the harsh world we live in. Of all the "one anothers" listed, mostly in the New Testament, Christ practiced every one. (He did not confess his sins; He had none; He took ours.) We can "one another one another." The one anothers are part of the essence, essentials of spiritual growth. The one anothers help us evaluate our own spiritual maturity as well as gauge where others are. Spiritual fruit as it ripens is much like the natural fruit we eat. It smells better and tastes better.

Maturing people exhibit sweet, maturing, spiritual fruit.

How we can help those we lead take the next step? How can relationships with others help them see Jesus and mature spiritually? Helping each other by being open and "getting out from behind the glass" means there will be some nervous moments. As you see friends follow Him, growing in His likeness and exhibiting more of the fruit of the Spirit, you will notice their words, their actions, and their character traits change for the better. When they look like Jesus, emulate them as they emulate Him. Ask yourself, what character traits are obvious and Christ-like? Which ones need to change for you to look more like Jesus? Be discerning. But how do I help someone know God, show them the change that has happened in my life, explain it using what God has written, see them receive it, and then change in it to look more like Christ? You can work through chapter seven's traits list with someone you trust to see how fruit can grow.

As I have changed over the years, I remember one incident which sticks in my mind above many others. I have to hold myself to be transparently accountably to my Lord, and deal with the tough things in my life. Jesus is the one who gets to point out to me, through His Spirit, where I need to change. And many times it is the last thing I want to hear. But Jesus points to the change in the heart which is not going to stay hidden from Him.

One day I was getting ready to help host a conference at a local hotel in Orlando. I saw Jay Strack, who was hosting "Leadership University" at the same hotel. (We knew each other from First Orlando.) He said, "Hey, come here, I want to show you something." He took me to the large conference room where he was about to speak to a couple hundred students. It was set up quite nicely. Conference tables all lined up perfectly. White linen tablecloths. Glass water pitchers at each table. Note pads and pens. And one large, fake, but very real looking frog at each person's spot on the table.

I asked, "What's that all about?" He then told me that in this session he would teach them that they must do the things that only they could do. They could not put those things on anyone else. The tasks or change in life which God shows them to do, they must do. No matter how tough the challenge. They must learn to do the hard things first. He said, "I tell them it's like eating a big live frog. Once you've done that, everything else that day will be easy."

I've never forgotten that. I needed to hear it.

Some things are huge and hard to change. Days when I ask Jesus that second question, "Jesus, what needs to change so I look more like You?" I am wanting to be transparent and accountable to Him. In that transparency He shows me things in my life and heart which must change. They may seem impossible. Yet my character traits must change for me to look more like Him. There are people I need to forgive. Attitudes which must be adjusted. Only I can do what He asks me. I cannot pass it off on someone else. I cannot blame someone else. I must own it. I must eat the big frog first. I must change.

It is possible for us to regularly exhibit the opposite of that Spiritual fruit. When we exhibit the opposites of the essentials of a spiritual relationship with God, we are showing where we need to grow. We are showing our lack of fruit in that area. The traits list in chapter seven explains that. He will guide us to how to know Him better, so we can look more like His Son. This habit of letting others in by becoming transparent … being transparent, is crucial to the next habit, Cultivating Community.

HABIT 4—CULTIVATING COMMUNITY.

This is learning as a fish to swim with your school of fish. Being with other believers and helping each other grow. The more transparent we are, the more authentic our community/group/ life becomes. Habit Three fits very well within this fourth habit. The more intentionally we focus on deepening our relationship with Christ (Habits One and Two) and then others (Habit Three), the more we relaxed we become as His children. This involves spending consistent, quality time in relationships centered around God and His Word, and the fruit of the Spirit He has given us. Practicing the "one anothers" we find in scripture should become natural. We become family.

Becoming family as a group was a different thought for me. Remember, I had been trained in how to develop numeric growth, not relational health. Quite a few summers ago I helped host a conference in Orlando. One of the men we asked to come teach some of our leaders was Leonard Sweet. He is a visionary and futurist. I had read one of his books, *AquaChurch*, and it challenged me.

During the time he met with us as a group I sensed we were asking questions which were becoming irrelevant. And he was answering questions we did not even know to ask…or even thoughts we should ask. I remember though that what he was saying did resonate with what was already going on in my heart, but I just didn't get it. It is a supreme struggle to believe you are doing exactly what you are supposed to … and doing nothing wrong … just doing very little right. But you thought you were. It is what you were taught. What you are currently doing to develop "church growth" will enable you to give numeric answers to your leaders as to how many, how often, and how many classes there are. The idea of family, and community, was becoming part of my thinking, but it was such a small part it went almost unnoticed. As leaders at that conference we were being challenged to think very differently. I had already started that process a few years back, but this seemed to be much more of a jump. One line from *AquaChurch*: "You can be right and be doing right things. But if your 'rightness' is not enveloped in an overwhelming embrace of love, your 'rightness' is wrong. Love is eternity based. The more you give, the more there is to go around" (p. 44). There was lot of discussion with our leaders after that. We needed to change. We needed to focus more on the community aspect. More on becoming good family.

The word community means different things to different generations. These days, it does not always mean the local grouping of people—the community you live in. To many people it has transformed to mean deepening relationship with others, building true koinonia/fellowship. Do you have community in your community? Are you connecting deeply to a small group who will help you move forward in Him? In these groups, we practice and live out all three questions and all six habits—all based on the Trinity we love.

Community can be a double-edged sword. The closer you get to one another, the less you sometimes allow others in. Glass walls evolve around you. Before you know it, you have created an aquarium where Habit Three cannot happen. New people become unwelcomed, accidentally.

People you meet out beyond the glass need something different. If what you offer in your church is the same as the world offers, people don't need it. They already have that. They already have acquaintances at work and around them, and distant relationships that don't work well. They may not be accepted out in their world. Also, if someone needs some religious habits to hang onto but doesn't make any relational changes, they are still the same as the world they live in. Nothing changes. It is redundant. Don't offer secularism—relationships slathered with some religious trappings. That is not based on what God has revealed to us in what He wrote.

Let me remind us, too much of the time we want a kingdom without the king. That way, we get to be king. Our community must be different. Our church must be different. It must represent something transcendent—relationships with God and others that draw people in and transform lives.

In defining "community," we use the words "quality time in relationships centered around the Word of God." This implies deepening relationships. Cultivating biblically deep relationships requires a deepening relationship with God, as well as with others.

A few years ago I was helping our church look for a church partnership in Wales. My first trip over there I got to spend some time with a young pastor. He had worked his way through Bible school and had been given an old church building to use to plant a church. It was the first plant in many years. Like many church buildings in Wales, it had been boarded up. At that time between one and two percent of the people in Wales were Christian. He started with a handful of people and God used him to grow the church from scratch.

He started a kids' club one afternoon a week at the church building. This went so well that a smaller church from another part of town asked if he could help them start one. He did.

Then another asked the same thing. He did, and he also started preaching there Sunday afternoons since they didn't have a pastor. There were only about twenty older ladies, but they were excited for the kids' club and for his preaching for them.

Then a fourth church asked if he could help them start a kids' club. So he did. That church building was magnificent. Imagine old wooden pews, stained glass, all about 175 years old. The building would hold about six hundred people. It was definitely one of the town's larger church buildings. They were running about forty on a high attendance day. And almost all of them were above the age of seventy-five. The preacher there was eighty-five years old and had been there for many years. He asked if the young pastor would start an afternoon kids' club for the "pensioners" (the elderly who were on pension). He said, "Not with the games, but a Bible study."

Let me back up. By the time I got to Wales, I had learned that there was a great revival or awakening around 1904. Reportedly 87 percent of the people were in church on Sunday mornings. Coal miners had come to Christ and stopped their cussing. They had to retrain the mules who helped bring the coal out of the mines to know what to do. True story! But from 1904 to 2014 Wales went from 87 percent believers to under 2 percent. There are so few Christians in Wales that the Welsh are considered an unreached people group. Such a serious decline in one hundred years. The great Welsh revival had a fatal flaw develop just after so many people came to Christ. They adopted the "attend church" approach to life. Go to church and the Vicar will tell you what you need to know about the Bible. So what I saw when I was there in that huge magnificent building was a small gathering—the final state of decline of the church in Wales with very few churches thriving.

I asked if I could go to the Bible study he had with the pensioners—all well over the age of seventy-five. The pastor of the church was there also. All of them had been members of that church since the late 1930s. They were a few of the children and grandchildren of the folks who came to Christ in the 1904 revival. Interestingly, all their relatives were buried out back. Almost every church in Wales is just like that. Hundreds and hundreds and hundreds of headstones in the back yard or side yard. And no parking lots. Because 175 years ago when those buildings were built there were of course no cars. So, just nice beautiful buildings with large graveyards. All filled with those who came to Christ during the great awakening of 1904.

When we got to the church the afternoon of the gathering, the pastor had me get a box of books out of the trunk of the car. He carried other boxes of materials. When we arrived in the parlor, there were about fifteen ladies and the pastor having tea and waiting. I had my tea and sat down. We passed out the books, which turned out to be Welsh Bibles. He taught in Welsh and then some in English so I could understand where they were. When we were finished, he collected the Bibles, put them back in the box and had me carry them back to put them in his trunk. I didn't think much of it. On the drive home though I asked him why he brought Bibles, and why didn't they bring their own Bibles. His answer still stuns me to this day. He said, "They don't have their own Bibles."

I sat there for a moment letting that sink in. I was not sure what he meant, so I said, "What?"

He said it again, "They don't have their own Bibles."

I know I looked odd as I asked the next question, "Why not?"

Derek said emphatically, "It's just *not done*."

"What?" I asked again.

He repeated, "It's just *not done*."

I was still not sure what he was saying, so I asked, "What's *not done?*"

To which he replied very emphatically and sternly, "People, especially the older ones, do not own their own Bibles ... it's just *not done.* You might get it wrong."

None of them had Bibles but him and the other Vicar. None of them. It's "just not done" that way. They never have had their own Bibles. Never. Ever. They were in their late seventies and had never, ever had a Bible of their own. Never. This is in Wales, not in a poor third world country. I could not wrap my mind around that. Still can't. The flaw after the great revival of 1904 was this— apparently, when they came to Christ, they all kept the tradition of the old Anglican churches where people thought only the Vicar could explain the Word well.

> All the new believers joined in the old traditions.
> ▬

All the new believers joined in the old traditions.

The Vicar should be the only one to handle "the Word" lest the people get it wrong. So, having their own copy of what God wrote was just *not done.* It was like I had been dropped somewhere in the past, prior to the reformation. And so, hundreds of people who came to Christ in the early 1900s went to the church buildings on Sunday, and never heard anything more about the Word until the next Sunday. And so on, and so on, and so on for one hundred plus years! No one had been discipling anyone since 1904. No small groups. No deep spiritual relational community. Just attendance awards. No one read a word from God's Word, besides what they had *heard* said on Sunday. And no one met to talk about their spiritual life. Ever. I still cannot believe what I heard. But it was all true.

All over Wales, the same habit of just coming to the church build-

ing to hear the Vicar. Year after year after year. Does any of this sound familiar?

A huge fishbowl experience. Then all the new believers just got in the bowl and assumed that is the way it was done. It "was" the way it was done. And they all slowly died off over the years. Never passing anything of Christ off to the next generation ... other than come sit with us on Sunday.

I suggested that we could get them Bibles and even put their names on them. It took us two years to convince him and them that it was ok to do that. Then a good friend of mine raised $2,000 to get them Bibles. The younger folks do have their own Bibles, but there are so few of them. It is mostly a country with very few believers, and very few of them are followers. Just now a few are wanting to make disciples. Many without their own copy of the Word of God. At least in the older churches. What came to my mind was, "No Word; no church."

> All over Wales, the same habit of just coming to the church building to hear the Vicar. Year after year after year. Does any of this sound familiar?

Habit Four is impossible without Habit One. In some places on the planet the written Word must be hidden from the government. But that makes their copy of the written Word, what God has said, even more valuable to them. On the other hand, in the West, we take it very lightly that we have our own copy. Probably more than a handful of copies.

To actually cultivate community, we have to be people who are getting to know God regularly and deeply together. Then being vulnerable about God and how He is transforming us. That will cultivate the relationships we are looking for. Otherwise it's just tea and crumpets.

HABIT 5—SERVING YOUR CIRCLE AND BEYOND

People who are mature, and are maturing, are those who give of themselves. They give of their possessions for the sake of others. Giving of ourselves is our spiritual service. Using our time, talent, and treasures as a gift to others is our privilege to help them become disciple-makers themselves. Knowing our spiritual gifts will help us serve where we will shine the most. Not that God does not ask you to serve or give in areas you may not be gifted in. Don't neglect your gift. It is for the body of Christ and beyond. This is a team effort within each small group and in the church as a whole. We all help shepherd one another. Yes, we are to serve as individuals. But being in a small group of people who do life together, and know each other's warts as well as successes, helps us serve well as a team. As we learn to serve each other as the body, we can get even better at serving beyond that circle into the world around us.

Quite a few years ago, I was privileged to be the co-President of Singles Pastors Metro. A yearly gathering of Singles Pastors from all the large Southern Baptist churches. Those were some great times with leaders of singles ministries with from a few hundred to a few thousand participants. We met once a year to discuss best practices and learn from each other about how we were doing ministry. A few of those years we were lucky enough to stay at Ritz Carltons. One of our guys had a side business as a travel agent and he found us some fairly cheap, or less expensive, prices. One year we were on Amelia Island on the coast of Florida. The few days we were there we had different guest speakers come address us on ministry topics. But that year, one of our keynote speakers had to cancel. The evening before, a few of the leaders were together discussing what we would do the next day to fill in that spot. One of them came up with a brilliant idea. Why not ask our assigned Conference Staff leader from the Ritz to address us about customer service? I can tell you having the blessing to stay at the Ritz, the service is stellar. We asked him and he said, "I am not one of you." To which we replied, "We don't care. You and your staff have been amazing at how you have served us. We should be this good as followers of Christ."

The next day he spoke for about twenty minutes. It was amazing. Here is the gist of what he said: Every morning, I gather all the staff who are working that shift. In a large room, they all stand in a single line facing me. They all know what is about to take place. At the Ritz, we have a card with all of the customer care essentials on it—about twenty of them. The whole staff has them memorized and they are to make certain they do every one of these for every guest, every day. The coordinator for that shift would then ask one person. He would pick one. "Sally, step forward, recite # 12, and tell us all how you accomplished that yesterday for one of our guests." (I wrote all this down. This is better than I have seen.) Each of their staff had to be ready to quote their core service principles, and how they had acted on that principle yesterday. I have read about this in other books, but I got to hear it and experience it from one of their great servants.

We began to use something similar at our church with staff. The questions you will find in the section "Intentionality must be intentional" are what we talked about as part of every staff meeting. We even had a whiteboard for it. On the left side of the whiteboard were the names of the leaders we oversee. On the right were stories of God at work in the lives of our leaders and their people. It was called the "Leaderboard" and a "Storyboard." We wrote relational stories of success on 3 x 5 cards and taped them to the storyboard. It is old school. We had yarn which we attached, one end next to the leader's name, and the other end next to the 3 x 5 card. So, yarn from one side of the board to the other.

Do we, in our own lives and the lives of those we may lead, effectively ask the right questions, intentionally looking for stories of grace and life change?

Do we even come close to taking the lives we live for Christ as seriously as the Ritz does as they serve their customers?

Let me tell you a story of a church in Nicaragua. The second poorest country in the western hemisphere. A great friend of mine, Mike Denton, leads a ministry called "Little Ones Ministries" (LOMKids.org). They seek to bring hope to poverty-stricken areas where even some of the most basic needs go unmet. "Hope Centers" feed kids and are now beginning to help adults learn a trade to gain employment. In the last two years, Pastor Ricardo at First Baptist Church in Corinto, Nicaragua has been discipling men. He is the pastor of one of the main churches we are helping there. He calls these men "Hombres de Valor" (Men of Valor).

It is much like what we are starting here in the states. "Mission Minded Men" are part of a group called "G300" (after Gideon's three hundred men). They want to be better disciples here, as well as to help Pastor Ricardo and others there. The church in Corinto, helped by our church, planted another church and built the building three years ago as well as one on a barrier island. Our church has helped them get started. But what God has done through Pastor Ricardo and now his men is amazing. Originally, he had started meeting with a large group of men to disciple them. It was during the week, not on Sunday. After COVID hit, they quit meeting in the large group and he started meeting with only about five men. Those five then each disciple about five others and so on. They are holding each other accountable, focusing on the "three questions," and trying to develop the "six habits."

We taught those to them two years ago. We are not taking credit here. But God does great things when you follow Him and obey. The "Men of Valor" are now helping more and more as some of them are now trained to build houses in three days for those in dire need. They have made the process even better. In America these houses would be more like a nice large shed. In Nicaragua they are the difference between having a home and living under a tarp and some plastic walls held together with rope. The families are then secure. House building and helping others is ramping up. One of the church buildings we helped them build was eaten by termites. So it was disassembled, and the good parts were used to build another house. At the same time, a small piece of property was obtained in the same area, and now has a metal structure and metal roof. They did the construction themselves. No walls, and a bare rough concrete floor for now. But the church is already meeting for worship there.

God is using the men and families to help not only each other in the church in Corinto, but to help them plant another church a few miles up the road. They are now looking to help yet another church plant a new church even further away. In the midst of all of this activity is discipling and seeing people come to Christ. People loving people daily in tangible ways, all the while discipling one another. They are serving in their circles and beyond. They do not have the programs or processes that we have. They only have each other and Christ. And that is enough. The joy I see on their faces when I am there reminds me that I am sometimes a whiny, spoiled American who puts his own comfort over serving others. But they are beyond their glass and don't even know it.

HABIT 6—GOING OUTSIDE.

Jesus left us with a life mission. We are sent. The Holy Spirit leads and sends us. There are so many who are far from Christ and need to know who we know.

Our mission for those who do not follow Christ is usually outside of our normal connections with those friends who already know Christ. Discipleship which is not evangelistic is not discipleship. Good news is always good. But all people are not always ready to hear it. All of us who are ready share in His mission of being the good news as we go. We patiently watch for those He drops in our paths to be the good news and also to tell it.

Let the Spirit guide you. He knows what He is up to.

I have gotten it wrong more than right. It is the mission of sharing the good news (the gospel) about who we know and love. Remember, it is not a text, but a Person. Loving the others in our lives so they can know this Person has love for them. As disciples we must consistently be encouraging one another to watch for those we can care for, invest in, and help draw near to Him. All the while, being an example of someone who loves Jesus and follows Him.

So much of the time we have left *going outside* to some professional sharers of good news. When actually, it is all our jobs. We do share the good news within our own church circles and within our groups about who Christ is. But we covered that in

Habits Three and Four and Five. Habit Six is mostly beyond our church and group gatherings, out there.

Let the Spirit guide you. He knows what He is up to.

Last Christmas Karen made her famous candied pecans. I swear she puts some addictive drug in them. Anyway, we packaged up a few bags, and even in COVID season I sensed God saying to take them to some neighbors. I sensed specifically two neighbors. It was New Year's Day when I got them delivered. I went to Jim and Cindy's house in the evening. They answered the door, and they both came to stand outside with me on the porch for ten minutes. Jim was in his short sleeve shirt freezing, but he had questions and wanted to talk.

When he was about frozen, he asked, "Could we have coffee sometime?"

"Sure," I said.

I felt a little tinge of guilt that I did not suggest it first. So, we scheduled it. The back story is this. I had been praying for Jim and Cindy since they moved in a couple of years earlier. We had a few pleasant but very short conversations as we crossed paths while dog walking. I had a sense that they might be a little nervous around me. Right or wrong, sometimes us pastors make people feel a little weird just because we are pastors. Like we have some direct conduit to God which is better than others, and our lives are perfect, and we don't sin or anything. Like all our prayers are perfect and they all get answered. As though we will all look like cherubs when we arrive in Heaven. All not true.

Anyway, Jim and I met for coffee, and he really wanted to know more about who God is, what the end times would look like, what God was up to in all the conspiracy theories and COVID stuff going around. We spent quite a bit of time talking. Jim was convinced he needed Christ to take more control of His life and specifically to give him some peace in all the anxiety. It was a great couple of hours at our kitchen over coffee. I believe Jim was already a follower at that moment. God has been working on him for some time. But he nailed some things down that day. He knows what God said about being "sealed by the Holy Spirit for the day of redemption" (Eph. 4:30).

Later that night he texted me and said his wife Cindy wanted to talk about what we had talked about. That happened. And now we are meeting regularly to watch "The Chosen." Karen and I are just walking with them as they get to know the heart of our great Father. Slowly becoming friends. Karen and Cindy are headed to a ladies' retreat later today. God is guiding us as we try to simply listen to his voice about those He has placed in the world around us. To love them. I'm not great at it, but I am trying to get better.

Living beyond the glass, it sometimes takes years to get to talk to someone about the important stuff. But just keep intentionally loving your neighbors even if it is mostly through your prayers, along with a few casual conversations.

Sometimes when you question God about your life and what is going to happen next, beyond the glass…He answers oddly. Also, God does not always answer as quickly as we would like when we ask. Sometimes we ask wrongly. Sometimes He says wait. Sometimes He says no. Then there are those times which are very rare, if ever.

One day while living in Orlando, I was in the back yard, intently questioning God while watering our new lime tree. I was deep in a state of pondering what He was wanting me to do next. I knew change in my life was coming. I could sense it. It was palpable. But I was clueless as to what it was to be. As I kept pouring the water on this lime tree, I was intensely in my own head, in my own mind. Wrestling with thoughts of failure, thoughts of opportunity, but mostly thoughts of hope and desire to be who God wanted me to be. I remember specifically saying, "God, what am I to do?"

Then, thud. Crunch. Something hit the roof of our house, bounced and landed in a pile of leaves over in the corner of the yard about fifteen feet from me. Out of the corner of my eye, I had only caught the movement as it landed in the leaves. I immediately thought it was some poor squirrel which had lost his grip in the tall oak tree right next to our house, and then got whopped senseless by the roof on his way to the pile of leaves on the ground. But it didn't move. Was it knocked out? Was it dead? Was it a squirrel? Our two dogs came slowly walking toward it, sniffing cautiously to figure out what this thing was. I put down the hose and kept my eye on the pile of leaves as I walked cautiously over to it. You can imagine, in my mind was this crazed squirrel which would gain consciousness about the time I got over there, and the "Mississippi Squirrel Revival" would play out in real time in my back yard.

Well, it wasn't a stunned squirrel. It was a fish. About ten inches long. Yep. I stood there with a look on my face you will get to see when we replay this video in heaven and God says to everyone, "Watch his face!!!"

Stuff happens sometimes. God speaks. I don't know what else to tell you. In that moment, when I had just asked, "God, what am I to do?" I sensed Him saying, "Doug...fisher of men!"

You think I'm making this up. I'm not. Comedy writers love to make up stories. But this one is true. A fish lands on the roof, then bounces to the ground right at the moment I asked God a question. As I thought about what had just happened, I realized an osprey had probably lost its grip on a fish. We lived close to a lake and there was a retention pond just behind our house. I did not see the osprey, but I did see the fish. I can relive that moment anytime I want. I can see the lime tree, the hose, the water, the dogs, the St. Augustine grass, the pile of leaves … and the fish. God answered my prayer. Not in a traditional way.

Most of the time the answers are simply a nudge on my soul, a sense in my Spirit of what He wants, or a scripture He reminds me of or guides me to. Sometimes it is a perfectly timed chapter in a book, or a blog I read. Sometimes it is a word from a friend who follows Christ, too. And yes, sometimes He says no, or not yet, or not now. But since I know Him and He has my best interest at heart, I trust Him. I was in a fishbowl and God was working to help me grab a hammer and get out.

What are you intently asking Him? Look for His answer. We are to always be fishers of men. That is being outside. That is beyond the glass. When you talk to God, there are things He will repeat again and again and again and again. Here are two: love Him and love others. Go fish! Everything you do will ultimately be about being "fishers of men." He wants your life to consistently be about Him and others as you go about work, school, raising a family, shopping, retirement … everything.

God does not do weird things regularly. At least not to my knowledge. He didn't use that burning bush experience with Moses, or anyone else, ever again that we know of. But I know that one day, He was telling me, "Fish for men. Look for people who are hurting and need Me."

Are you going outside? … beyond the glass? I wish I could tell you that I became great at going outside from that moment on. I did not. I do however write it here. I attempt to keep my eyes open for those who need Him. They are everywhere. "Whoever is of God hears the words of God" (John 8:47). He is speaking to you. Do you hear Him? Jesus said, "'Those who are well have no need of a physician, but those who are sick. I came not to call the righteous, but sinners" (Mark 2:17).

Going outside is mostly about paying attention to the Spirit as you live your life. Hearing His words toward you concerning others. It is by far *not* the only thing He says to us. But concerning going outside, we must hear Him as He directs us to others. Intently watching for people you can invest in. Even if it is for just a moment.

Let me tell you how one of my pastors did this. It is only one way of investing in those who are not a part of church. In 2004 when I was at First Orlando, Jim Henry was the senior pastor. I had just moved from being the Singles Pastor to the Equipping and Education Pastor. It was a big jump for me. I had lots of ideas and we put a team together to integrate all processes and programs to make them work well together, as well as connecting all of that to each of our small groups. It was a massive undertaking but well worth the time and tears and arguments. One item which was daunting was to make as certain as possible that we had done everything we could to see the myriad of guests get connected to a small group. We made phone calls, emails, even designing a system way back then into which we loaded all info before we even left the campus. Then we assigned those guests to leaders in specific LifeGroups via email so they could make immediate contact and invite them to lunch.

We were a regional church and had people coming from a 45-minute radius. That meant we could have people who live an hour-and-a-half apart. So, we wanted to do our best to get them connected to a potential group of friends as soon as possible. We even tried to match proximity of home address to the leader they were assigned to. These people had come to us from the outside. We must get them to a group of friends. In the midst of all this I found out that Jim Henry had been making phone calls to guests for two hours on Monday evenings as far back as anyone could remember. Now keep in mind, at that time he had been the pastor there for 25 years. And at the time we were having attendance of over 6,000 on a Sunday. Yet, the senior pastor of a church that size would call guests just to say thanks for being at one of our worship services. And he would ask how he could pray for them. Going outside means at least starting a conversation with the guest who shows up at any gathering. Jim also would engage in conversation with anyone he could. I remember one story about a guy at the car wash whom he had become friends with. Jim went outside!!!

Going outside means so much more than responding to guests. A good friend, Jason Dukes, wrote a book titled *Live Sent*. It is about just that. "You are a letter," Paul says in 2 Corinthians 3:2-3.

You are *sent*. Are you going? Are your eyes open to the people in your life? Do you see them? Do you really see them as souls in need of Christ or better deep relational knowledge of Christ? You are sent each and every day. But are you going?

Jesus sent the Spirit (John 14:26). Now the Spirit sends/ leads you. He sends. He guides. He holds the map of Ephesians 2:10: "For we are his workmanship, created in Christ Jesus for good works, which God prepared beforehand, that we should walk in them." He knows the works we have to do tomorrow. He has planned them for you. And they involve people. The spiritual works we do are "as we go." But He doesn't always guide us to the easiest of assignments.

My best friend, Mark Lambert, and I wrote a book called

How God Asks You to Love Others. The whole point of the book is learning to sense the "tap on the shoulder" of the Spirit as He asks you to help someone, to invest in someone's life—whether it is just a moment or more, it is for eternity. Mark has said at breakfast meetings more than once that God just wants you to, "Show up, on purpose, with your eyes open."[12] The book speaks for itself. It is a short, very pointed read, with lots of stories and very little structured "how to." It is life on purpose.

We are sent. Are you going?

The Spirit sent the apostle Paul far away to the Gentiles (Acts 22:21). The Spirit prevented Paul from speaking in Asia. He forbade him from doing so. The Spirit led him and his troop of men around to Mysia and as they tried to enter Bithynia, the Spirit of Jesus did not allow them

We are sent. Are you going?

to go in. Instead, Paul had a dream in which a man from Macedonia was asking them to come help them. And Paul absolutely knew it was God who was calling them there.

The Spirit will guide you to those in whom He wants you to invest. Whether that is for ten minutes or a lifetime. Keep your heart open to where He guides you.

---

[12]Mark Lambert and Doug Dees, *How God Asks You to Love Others* (Murrell's Inlet, South Carolina: Covenant Books, 2020), 33.

SEVEN

As You Are Going

"**A**s you are going" means all the time. As you are going about your life ... as you meet with others at the church building...everywhere. All of your waking moments. As you gather with others in the church building or during your other waking hours, you are to help whoever He tells you to, to help them out of their fishbowl experience. All habits are "as you are going" habits. Make them your own habits. They are relational habits which are to work out in your life and the life of your church. Connecting to the Trinity and to others "as you are going" involves a participle, "as you are go-ing." This is not a suggestion from Jesus, it is connected to an imperative verb in the Great Commission. Whatever words you use to explain this, make certain they reflect the heart of our Father. We are suggesting that you do not start with a function or a form, or a strategy with numerical increase as an end goal. All those are fine and good. If you remember nothing else, remember this:

God existed in relationships before time. He started with relationships in the garden; He ends with relationships in eternity. His highest goals start and end with relationships here,

*and now, and later. Get to know and love Him, and get to
know and love others, before you design all other forms and
functions.*

"Therefore go," or "as you are going" is at the heart of each
of the three relational questions, and the six habits are not to
be thought of as only time slots or specific places. But don't
forsake gathering together on purpose. Jesus was often interrupted "as He was going" to a certain place. Paul continually had instances he had not planned. But he was intently going "as he went" where he was sensing the Spirit lead. I can't stress enough that the three relational questions and six habits are for "all the time in all places ... as you are going," and as you are praying.

God existed in relationships before time. He started with relationships in the garden; He ends with relationships in eternity. His highest goals start and end with relationships here, and now, and later. Get to know and love Him, and get to know and love others, before you design all other forms and functions.

It is what Jesus wanted us to do when He said those words
that Matthew recorded. The "as you are going" started for those
apostles right then and there. And "as you are going" has never
stopped. "Go, and as y'all are going" is a participial phrase with
a plural subject. The "y'all" is the southern American plural
version. For the Northerners reading, it would be "yous guys."
Jesus wanted them all, and us, to know that from now on: "Go,
you are to go, and as you are going, all y'all ... make disciples."

Every moment of every day you are connected to the Trinity. Some days you feel more connected than others. But They never shift or change. They will keep you moving. Your interaction with others is a cause and result of your life becoming more and more of the abundant life Christ desires for you.

Your car is a great example of this. There are three fluids which make it all keep moving. You must have gas, oil, and water. All three play a very important role all the time. If one has a problem, the whole car has a problem. (If you have an electric car, you are going to have to come up with your own analogy.) And the six habits are like the six cylinders in your car. They all are to work all the time, in concert. Three questions, six habits, as you are going.

INTENTIONAL AND SERENDIPITOUS

This Kingdom we live in is not ours. It is the Kingdom of our King Jesus. He knows what He is doing, and He knows what He is planning to do in it—for His sake and the sake of those He loves. So why not let His Spirit guide you? Life is not just a process. Though processes are good. The Spirit knows where Christ is at work, so why not let Him lead you? It must be both intentional and serendipitous. Jesus both purposed to do things and was also interrupted as He was heading to do them.

People you intend to disciple are important. And those with whom you only get a minute or two in life are important also. Think about how many times Jesus was interrupted as He was on His way. Think about how many times we see Him telling His disciples to meet Him somewhere.

Imagine if you had $1,000 to intentionally invest. Imagine those dollars were minutes. One thousand minutes. You have more waking minutes in a week, but let's start with one thousand. Who has God, the Spirit, led you to invest in? To spend intentional time with to help them with life and to mature in the

Lord. Are you taking sixty of those minutes to talk to someone personally, over lunch about how they are doing? Are you taking some of those minutes to take someone with you as you go help somebody with an issue or a burden or a chore? Do they see you in life being a disciple who follows Jesus and does as He does? Do you have any minutes spent with someone who works down the hall from you or in the next cubicle or is working on the car next to the one you are repairing? In the midst of conversation, you sense them in a down mood. You ask what's up. You could spend five minutes and make a huge difference by genuinely caring for someone by asking a simple question. You find out their mother is not doing well. Offer to pray for them. Show some of the fruit of compassion. Come back the next day and ask them how she is doing. Maybe you have ten minutes each day invested in that person. You may be the only person who cared enough to ask, or stop and talk, or pray, or go back and show compassion. You never know what those ten minutes will do. If you need to, go to the hospital and see their mom. Take someone with you that you are intentionally discipling. The Spirit can and will lead you in all this. What small group are you in with others who can also pray for this situation? All of this is moving people forward by you showing them love, and what Christ looks like. The old WWJD bracelet still holds true. Think about *What Would Jesus Do*, then do that! In your listening to the Spirit, He will consistently guide you. Where are all your thousand minutes spent? Some could be in prayer for those people.

Every "who" has a "where," and every "where" has a "who."

This is not a Dr. Seuss reference. But no matter where you go, there you are … and there are people most everywhere. Look for them. In asking the three questions to God, remember,

God is sovereign. Jesus is wherever you go, and His Holy Spirit lives in you, so He is with you wherever you go. Since you are wherever you go, your character change can and should happen everywhere.

People are everywhere you go. The question then becomes, who is it that you are to invest in? Where does that happen? Who is the Spirit leading you to? Refer to the one thousand minutes above. God can also call you to a specific people group. He might call you to help middle schoolers. He might call you to help babies and their parents. He might call you to help adults who are homeless. He might call you to help specific neighbors. He might call you to another nation. My friend Mike Denton of LOM-Kids.org uses disciple-making methods and multiplying disciples and churches in other nations. God might call you to work with senior adults, or those in a nursing home.

> Every "who" has a "where," and every "where" has a "who".

You get the picture. People are everywhere. Every "who" has a "where." The question then becomes, "Who are your 'whos'?" Who is it (singular and plural) that God is asking you to invest in, to help follow Jesus? One minute, five minutes, sixty minutes. It really is that simple.

But you have to move in and be intentional to do it. You have to break the glass, and maybe take some fish with you. You may need to work within the glass to get others outside the glass. How do they need help? God will show you. All the while, you are helping them to answer the first two questions for themselves.

Investing in people may be a very short few minutes all the way to a lifetime of discipling someone. If you want to see people grow, you must invest in them. If you open a savings account or 401K, it will not grow unless you first put something in. It is the same with people. You go first. Ask God the third question, and watch Him start showing you things in your life. He most likely has already been showing you people, but your eyes were not wide open yet to see.

It is important to be able to explain in words that you know who Christ is, and how He became and is becoming Lord of your life. In 1 Peter 3:15 God says, "Always being prepared to make a defense to anyone who asks you for a reason for the hope that is in you." That hope is based on His holiness and you can, as His child, talk about how the hope in Him has changed your life. God wrote, "What then is Apollos? What is Paul? Servants through whom you believed, as the Lord assigned to each. I planted, Apollos watered, but God gave the growth" (1 Cor. 3:5-7). We all do our part because we love Him for giving us hope.

THE ENEMY HATES INTENTIONALITY

You were born related to him. John 8 tells us that. We had Satan as our father. Also, "We were born dead in our trespasses and sin" (Eph. 2:1). But God in His great mercy has given us a way of escape.

The enemy will fight you at every turn. He wants to stop you, to keep you from asking any of the three questions, and to stop you from hearing God's answers. He will attempt to thwart anything that looks like the six habits. He comes to steal, kill, and destroy, but Christ comes to give life abundantly (John 10:10). And we have armor to wear. We should put that armor on daily. The armor is made of Christ, and Ephesians 6 tells us to armor up as we go about our lives. Attempt to break the glass and live free. Satan and his minions will do all they can to box you back up and tell you that you have no business outside the glass. But you do! Your business is imitating our Lord. Jesus came to set the captives free. As you are free, help Him free others.

If the enemy can't steal, kill, or destroy you and the things of God in your life, he will try to injure you. He will work to win any battle or skirmish. He will distract or try to rattle you. "This is the spirit of the antichrist, which you heard was coming and now is in the world already. Little children, you are from God and have overcome them, for he who is in you is greater than he who is in the world" (1 John 4:3-4).

One of the doctoral seminars I got to take was Biblical Preaching with Dr. R. C. Sproul. Just the thought of sitting in a room with him and about twelve other men for 40 hours in one week caused my stomach to churn. I was nervous. That week each of us was to preach for a ten-minute time slot. He would tell us each day who was up tomorrow. We then were to go home that night and prepare a sermon. It had to have all the parts—opening, conclusion, points, illustrations and transitional sentences. The next day we had to preach it with no text, no notes, no Bible. Nothing. And all in ten minutes. Thinking of standing there naked before God and the other guys and Dr. R.C. Sproul. I was terrified.

On Wednesday, he said the next day was my turn. I went home, prayed, and prepared. That next morning once we finished some opening items, Dr. Sproul said, "Dees, you're up."

So, as my stomach turned to soup, I stood up and headed to the podium as he walked to his chair in the back corner of the small classroom. He sat down, and as I was about to start, he said, "You know Dees, I was going to use you as an example of how to dress until you wore that ugly tie."

I stood there panicked. I could hear my stomach. It was not happy. But did I actually hear Dr. Sproul say that? I looked down at my tie. And sure enough, it did not go with my suit at all. It was clearly the wrong tie. Apparently, I was so nervous I did not even think about it. Then, at that moment, a clear way out came to me. I remembered a story that my pastor had told me about a similar situation which had happened in the class he was in with Dr. Sproul a few years ago. So, after about a five second pause, I said, "R.C. …" (the guys in the class looked at me in disbelief, like the two lawyers looked at Tom Cruise as he was about to address Jack Nicholson in the movie *A Few Good Men* … they were saying don't go there). I said, "R.C., I heard a story about a guy a few years ago who wore a clip-on tie in this class. You went up to him, pulled that clip-on tie off, tied it in a knot, and went to the door and threw it outside." (By this time Dr. Sproul was smiling, and I mean a huge smile.) I said, "You then told him, 'Never wear a clip-on tie! It's not long enough to cover your belly, and you look like a clown. And nobody believes a clown when they talk about Jesus.'" Then I bowed my head and started to pray out loud before my sermon, "Father, bless us as we are about to hear from Your Word." I could hear Dr. Sproul holding back laughter during the prayer. When I finished praying, I looked up. He was smiling that huge toothy, genuine smile he had. Then I preached my ten-minute sermon. He was trying to rattle me. He succeeded.

One of the points he made that week was this: every time you get up to preach or teach, or talk to anyone on God's behalf, the enemy will try to rattle you so that you do not deliver what you know about our great God. Among the many things I learned from that great and godly man that week was that people and the enemy will try to distract you in any way they can when you are about to speak about our Father. Whether it is a sermon or with an individual person. You must get past being rattled, or fearful, or forgetful. You must not let anything get in the way of communicating exactly what you know to be true about who He is. The best way to do that? ... Know Him as a Person, and know He is there.

Know He is with you, and you are talking about a friend, who is your God. He is a Person. Get to know Him, then tell others what you know about Him, as a Person they can know also. What you have to say about Him, your story, is unique, and is designed by God not only to be deeply precious to you as the story of Him and you, but to be an inspiration to others who may not know they have a story. It may be for others to see how their story can grow as they get to know our great Father. The Sprit will lead you to tell your story out there. And the enemy will hate that intentionality.

After Jesus' baptism where the Spirit, was "descending like a dove" (Matt. 3:16), that same Spirit lead Jesus into the wilderness to be tempted by Satan. The enemy was not going to win. But from what we can tell, this was the beginning of the battle with Jesus. Jesus would show who He was, and who He is! Jesus now walks with you through whatever experience you have. Look to Him when the enemy attacks and flaming arrows are flying.

In the Old Testament God Himself also allows tough things to happen in life. Things that rattle us to the core. He brings up Job's name to Satan. Thanks, God. But God knows what He is doing. Through some horrible circumstances Job ends up knowing God better than he did at the beginning of the book. Remember, we are to "know Him and love Him more." How many lives has Job helped through his story of remaining a godly man even in horrible circumstances? He has helped many who are "outside." Habit One and Habit Six, we go with the One who loves us.

STAYING BEYOND THE GLASS—THE PROCESS

There will always be the tendency to go back behind the glass. To retreat. To hide. The enemy hates it when you get out. He hates it that you may affect others.

If you lead a church, start first with your staff, then leaders, then everyone in the church. If the pastors and staff of a church do not model "living beyond the glass," it will just be a program and will soon fade. If you do model it, you will affect your leaders and those they lead. And in time, the whole church. This is about the only strategic structure I will suggest. But make certain you ask this of every staff member, ever leader, every event, every program, every process, every group, every care group. Everything. You must attempt to get this DNA in all parts of the church. Remember the story about the little boy putting the cut-up paper together —you must put the man together for the world to come together. Here are the three questions and the six habits again:

Three questions—

- Father, how can I know You and love You better?
- Jesus, what needs to change so I look more like You?
- Spirit, who are You leading me to invest in?

Six habits:

- Finding the Person of God
- Immersing in Him

- Getting Out Lets Others In
- Cultivating Community
- Serving Our Circle and Beyond
- Going Outside

Intentional Disciple-Making Questions for Staff:
Staff/leader questions to themselves-

- How am I asking the three questions to myself daily?
- How am I developing the six habits on my own daily?

Ask your staff/leaders—in light of the 3 questions and 6 habits:

- What leaders have you met with in the last week/month?
  - » What questions did you ask them?
  - » How are they doing spiritually?
    - › Are they getting to know the Father and love Him better? How?
    - › What character change is needed? How are they doing with that?
    - › Who are they investing in specifically? Name them.
  - » How are you praying for them?
  - » How are those they lead doing spiritually?
    - › How are they getting to know the Father and love Him better?
    - › What character trait change is needed?
    - › Who are they investing in specifically?
    - › (For students, children, preschool—do your leaders also know where their parents are spiritually?)

» What are they doing for those in their groups to help them?

» Who are they apprenticing?

- How are you helping them with the above? (Example: Are you willing to go with a leader or a member for a coffee or lunch to meet with someone?)

IN GROUPS:

- Are they working at getting to know the Father through what He has written?
- Are they learning to immerse themselves in Christ—to abide in Him?
- Are they genuinely helping one another change in character to more Christlikeness?
- Are they doing what it takes to cultivate community?
- Are they learning how the Spirit has gifted them, and are they using those gifts?
- Are they helping each other to look for those who are far from Christ?

CRUCIAL: A staff should be an example of a community. We should be actively cultivating that community as we seek to be disciples who are disciple-makers. Our character should be changing to look like Jesus. We also have an organization chart, and as an employee you cannot come and go as you please. You have a job within the community which is for the sake of the community at large, the people of your local church. So, as a disciple-maker, your first job is to be an example of a growing disciple within your community. The second is your technical job description. To the degree you all grow together and exhibit the spiritual relational habits, you will lead the people of your church well. You must lead by example.

THE PROCESS:
Do all we can to get people connected to a small group

Small groups on Sunday morning—

- These usually last about an hour.
- The Bible is taught/discussed in ways that God is known more deeply.
- The "Three Questions" are at least addressed/noted on different levels per week.
- Focus on the "Six Relational Habits of a Disciple-Maker"—are they habits?
- Not all that happens can happen in that one hour. You must move beyond the hour.
- Find ways to deepen the six relational habits during the week.

Small groups during the week—

- They usually last over two hours. Focus on deepening the "Six Essential Habits."
- Ask the "Three Questions."

A weekday small group can be made up of—

- Members of a LifeGroup who want more time together.
- Those who cannot make Sunday morning regularly.
- Friends who may not attend a church yet.
- Seasoned disciples who could help mentor.

- Those who might not be ready yet to attend church.

One more Ritz Carlton story. We got to stay at the Ritz at Laguna Nigel in Southern California. One day I was at the pool with my wife. A waiter came over and said, "Is there anything you need, sir?"

I paused, then said, "I would really like a Dr. Pepper."

He said, "It would be my pleasure." (I think I know where Chick-fil-A got that.)

After some time, I thought he had forgotten. That is not like service at the Ritz-Carlton. But a few minutes later he came back with my Dr. Pepper in a big glass. As he started to leave, I said, "You seem to be a little out of breath."

He said, "Yes sir. We don't have Dr. Pepper at the Ritz. I had to go down to Walgreens to get it for you."

I about dropped the Dr. Pepper. I told the young man I would be telling his supervisor what an incredible job of serving he had done. That young man was probably hoping he would be called on the next day to step forward and tell the Dr. Pepper story.

Again, I ask, "Do we even come close to taking the lives we live for Christ as seriously as the Ritz takes service for their customers?"

Being intentional is imperative. As the church, we can and should focus on shifting what we do to more of a relational intent. Read *DiscipleShift* by Jim Putman. Visit DiscipleShift.org and go to a training. There are so many great things going on right now in the worldwide body of Christ. Why would you want to stay the way you are—stuck behind the glass?

The next few sections are simply lists of traits, exercises, one–anothers, terminology, and what we are doing at my church now. But don't stop reading. There is one more page after the lists.

TRAITS

SOME CHARACTER TRAITS/FRUIT and OPPOSITES: (some are listed as fruit—all are from God)

Too much of the time the enemy gets us to live in the left column. He gets us to think and act opposite to what God desires. But we can take every thought captive and make it obedient to Christ (2 Cor. 10:5).

Dead in sin	Alive in Christ	We are first fruit	Eph. 2:1, 8, 9
Unrighteous	Righteous	Living according to Christ	Psa. 11:7
Curt	Kind	Gentle toward others	Gal. 5:22
Bad	Good	Actions/words	Jas. 4:17
Anxiety	Peaceful	Temper/mood	Phil. 4:5-7
Taker	Giver	Money/talents/time	Matt. 25:15-28
Hateful	Loving	Expect nothing in return	Gal. 5:22
Sad	Joyful	Outlook on life	Gal. 5:22
Insistent	Patient	Willingness to wait	Gal. 5:22
Undisciplined	Self-controlled	You control yourself	1 Cor. 9:25
Prayerless	Prayerful	Concern for God and others	1 Thess. 5:17
Unforgiving	Forgiving	Throw away the wrong	Col. 3:13
Pride	Humility	Not exalting yourself	Luke 14:11
Selfish	Selfless	Treat others as important	Phil. 2:3
Harsh	Gentle	Calming situations	Prov. 15:1
Disregarding	Compassionate	Genuine caring	Col. 3:12
Captive	Pardoned	Set free to love	Isa. 55:6,7
Bad reputation	Good reputation	Known as the real you	1 Tim. 3:7
Uneasy	Comforted	Relieved and relaxed	2 Cor. 1:3-4

Below are four character traits/one anothers. We cannot take people where we have not been. So we must first seek our Father to know Him, abide in Christ, and ask Christ to show us where we need to grow in His character. We cannot just explain a character trait to others about Him, we must show it to them. But first, the Spirit will convict us that we need it.

Ask yourself about just these four traits:

Do you need change from being **curt** to more **kind**?

- Have you experienced God's kindness toward you?
- It is a spiritual fruit (Gal. 5:22).
- "Or do you presume on the riches of his kindness and forbearance and patience, not knowing that God's kindness is meant to lead you to repentance?" (Rom. 2:4-5).
- Do you see His kindness toward you?
- Is this kindness something you then portray to others, and tell them about His kindness?
- Do others see this fruit in your relationship with Him?

Do you need to change from being **insistent** to **patient**?

An impatient man cannot explain biblical patience very well until he has experienced it, grown in it, and can show it. Otherwise his words are hollow. His actions betray his definitions/explanations of the word patience (1 Cor. 13:4).

- Have you experienced God's patience with you?
- Have you learned how to be more patient with yourself?
- Have you exhibited patience toward others?
- Even the smallest amount of patience can be shown and explained to someone who has less patience than you.

Do you need to change from being **anxious** to being more **peaceful**?

Even the smallest amount of peace can be helpful to someone who has more anxiety than you and less peace than you (Phil. 4:4-9).

- Have you experienced God's peace?
- Have you been peaceful in tough situations?
- Have you exhibited peace among others during a time of great trial?

Do you need to change from being **uneasy** to being **comforted**, and then to comfort others?

- Have you experienced God comforting you?
- Have you learned how to accept comfort from Him?
- Have you been able to comfort someone with the comfort God has given you?
- Can you explain what comfort is and where it comes from?
- Now you are ready to show it and explain it more.
- Even the smallest amount of comfort can be of great help to someone in need (2 Cor. 1:3,4).

Which of God's traits comes to your mind? Do not wait till you think you have all His traits all together in all areas to start to be open to the Spirit leading you to people who need help. If you have Him living inside you, you have what it takes to help someone move forward.

Let Him pick who. Then respond by moving into that relationships to help them see Him more clearly and become more like Him in character. Then they can help someone else move forward. You can only share what you have. Where do you get more fruit? From Him. In what God wrote about that characteristic/fruit, show a person where you received that fruit. They can and should then go to Him to get more of that fruit. As you give it away, God will replenish your supply.

EXERCISES

In a relational training session, these exercises can explain to leaders what relational change looks like for question two. Ask them to let the Holy Spirit guide them in their answers, rather than giving "Sunday school answers" they know ahead of time.

TRAINING TIME:

SMALL GROUP TIME 1—Pick from the list of fruit/ change.

Take a few minutes to describe:

- How you came to know that character/fruit exists.
- In whom have you seen that character/fruit?
- How has Jesus encouraged you to change so you bear that fruit?
- Who do you know who needs to see and understand that character/fruit?
- Will you show it to them?

Sometimes we learned character in our minds but did not have it travel to our hearts. We have hoarded what little character we have for fear we would not get more, or others would not understand or want it. We have not gone to others because we thought we had to explain something and explain it well. What if you were supposed to show character long before you explain it? What if people want to be loved instead of informed?

Let me illustrate. It's Valentine's day and a delivery man shows up at the door. The wife answers the door. The delivery man says to the wife, "I am here to inform you, via candy, flowers, and a card, that your husband, sitting over there in his recliner, loves you. He ordered all this online for you." She then kisses him and goes and gets in the delivery truck. She is riding off with him.

Technically, the man in the recliner celebrated Valentine's Day. But it was not from the heart. Heart matters. People want to be cared for, not just informed or have love delivered.

SMALL GROUP TIME 2—

- Pick a person in the group (someone you know).
- Pick a character trait/fruit you have seen in them.
- Verbally encourage them by saying, "I have seen you grow in_____ character or 'one another' and it is obvious you have become more like Christ. I appreciate that about you."
- Take turns until everyone has had a chance to speak.
- Each person: List three people you know in your small group for whom you need to do this.
- Each person: List three people you know outside your group, and the church, for whom you need to do this. Let the Holy Spirit guide you to them. OR to whom do you need to go and show them what comfort looks like? What concern looks like? What genuine care looks like? What fruit do they need to know about? Will you deliver it?

Questions for leaders:

- Do you know if all those in your small group are believers?
- Do you know where all those in your small group are spiritually?
- What can you do to help them move forward toward Jesus?
- In what way could you encourage them in character change you have seen?
- Who can you use to help you do that?
- Who is your apprentice?
- How would your group make certain that you all are asking the three questions and developing the six habits?

ONE ANOTHERS
The One Anothers of the New Testament
How are we doing these with each other? Do we just know them, or do we exhibit spiritual relationships with them?

- Be at peace with each other (Mark 9:50).
- Wash one another's feet (John 13:14).
- Love one another (John 13:34, 35; 15:12, 17).
- Be devoted to one another in brotherly love (Rom. 12:10).
- Honor one another above yourselves (Rom. 12:10).
- Live in harmony with one another (Rom. 12:16).
- Love one another (Rom.13:8).
- Stop judging one another (Rom. 14:13).
- Accept one another, just as Christ accepted you (Rom. 15:7).
- Instruct one another (Rom. 15:14).

- Greet one another with a holy kiss (Rom. 16:16).
- When you come together to eat, wait for each other (I Cor. 11:33).
- Have equal concern for each other (I Cor. 12:25).
- Greet one another with a holy kiss (I Cor. 16:20).
- Greet one another with a holy kiss (II Cor. 13:12).
- Serve one another in love (Gal. 5:13).
- If you keep on biting and devouring each other, you'll be destroyed by each other (Gal. 5:15).
- Let us not become conceited, provoking and envying each other (Gal. 5:26).
- Carry one another's burdens (Gal. 6:2).
- Be patient, bearing with one another in love (Eph. 4:2).
- Be kind and compassionate to one another (Eph. 4:32).
- Forgiving each other (Eph. 4:32).
- Speak to one another with psalms, hymns and spiritual songs (Eph. 5:19).
- Submit to one another out of reverence for Christ (Eph. 5:21).
- In humility consider others better than yourselves (Phil. 2:3).
- Do not lie to each other (Col. 3:9).
- Bear with each other (Col 3:13).
- Forgive whatever grievances you may have against one another (Col. 3:13).
- Teach one another (Col. 3:16).
- Admonish one another (Col. 3:16).
- Make your love increase and overflow for each other (I Thess. 3:12).
- Love each other (I Thess. 4:9).
- Encourage each other (I Thess. 4:18).

- Build each other up (I Thess. 5:11).
- Encourage one another daily (Heb. 3:13).
- Spur one another on toward love and good deeds (Heb. 10:24).
- Encourage one another (Heb. 10:25).
- Do not slander one another (Jas. 4:11).
- Don't grumble against each other (Jas. 5:9).
- Confess your sins to each other (Jas. 5:16).
- Pray for each other (Jas. 5:16).
- Love one another deeply, from the heart (I Pet. 3:8).
- Live in harmony with one another (I Pet. 3:8).
- Love each other deeply (I Pet. 4:8).
- Offer hospitality to one another without grumbling (I Pet. 4:9).
- Each one should use whatever gift he has received to serve others (I Pet. 4:10).
- Clothe yourselves with humility toward one another (I Pet. 5:5).
- Greet one another with a kiss of love (I Pet. 5:14).
- Love one another (I John 3:11, 23; 4:7, 11, 12).
- Love one another (II John 5).

TERMINOLOGY

These are some disciple-making terms. You choose how you define yours based on scripture.

- We who have accepted Christ as Lord and Savior are **believers**. The word believer is a noun (Rom. 10:9, 10).
- Every believer is to be a **disciple**. It is also a noun. A follower of Jesus who exhibits an example of Jesus—His character, His attitude, His actions, His methods, as we

go. What we learn, of Him and His ways, we should put into practice. Brandon Guindon says, "The truth is that a follower of Jesus can grow as a disciple yet never become a disciple-maker."[13] Spiritual growth is required to become a disciple-maker.

- Every disciple is to be a ***disciple-maker***. The only time the word is an imperative verb is in Matthew 28:19. As we help others see Jesus by exhibiting these character traits and letting people know it is Him causing the change, we can explain how He has changed us. In doing so, we help others follow Him (Matt. 4:19). Jesus is the only one who ever used this as an imperative verb—and He sent his disciples to be disciple-makers. That was then, but He is still discipling us, so that verb is expected of us too.

- Some will be ***lead disciple-makers***. This is someone who leads a group to follow Christ well in this way. An apprentice is someone who is training for this lead role. 2 Timothy 2:2 says, "What you have heard from me in the presence of many witnesses entrust to faithful men who will be able to teach others also." This is a great explanation of four generations of disciple-makers in one verse. Not everyone can or should lead a group. But everyone can be a disciple-maker. The early church met from house to house. That is a lot of disciple-making. Paul led Timothy to be one of these, and then to lead the church.

- A few could be ***disciple-making coaches.*** This is someone who leads those who lead groups. And helps start many groups. Paul was one of these. He planted churches, coached leaders, and raised up leaders. Acts

---

[13] Brandon Guindon, *Disciple-Making Culture* (Brentwood, TN: HIM Publications, 2020), 19.

14:23 says, "And when they had appointed elders for them in every church, with prayer and fasting they committed them to the Lord in whom they had believed."

MY CHURCH

Currently at the church I serve, First Moore Baptist Church, we have an amazing work of God happening. God called a new pastor last year, Charlie Blount. His desires to see disciple-making happen were like throwing gas on a fire. As a staff we had spent the last few years working toward implementing some things we found in *DiscipleShift* by Jim Putman, and what we learned in training with Real Life Discipleship, led by Brandon Guindon. We now realize we were laying tracks for the train to run on. Charlie has led us to define our desires for disciple-making in some simple yet deep focuses. We want to Know, Follow, and Become like Jesus. That means we are "relational," "imitational," and "transformational." There are three questions we use to focus on those three characteristics:

- How does God want me to know Him more?
- What is God asking me to do for Him and others?
- What has God revealed in me that needs to change?

These three help us stay focused on the following E's:

- Exalt the Father—Worship
- Equip the saints—Discipleship
- Embrace one another—Community
- Empower the body—Service
- Engage the lost—Missions

Here is the amazing thing—God gave Charlie this vision for moving the church forward before he came to us. You can't imagine how high my soul leaped when I heard him explain that vision when he arrived.

So, what is God doing in your midst? What questions are you asking? What relationships are you building? What do you think Jesus meant when He said go?

CONCLUSION:

The three questions and six habits—if we make them all relational habits—will propel us forward into deepening spiritual relationships with God and others. We do not have to remain as we are. We can be more like Him and become more of who He desires us to be. We do not have to repeat any missteps and mistakes we have made in the past. If we devote ourselves to the Trinity as They have devoted Themselves to us, we will be used by God to see our life changed, and then the lives of others changed.

As you intentionally look for opportunities to help others, you will find ways within your relationships to multiply the life and character of Christ. They will hear and see you as you walk like Him.

This takes time. It does not happen with only one hour on Sunday or only in a small group. Therefore, we suggest you find other times and places to meet and discuss God's Word to help each other grow in the character of Christ and follow the Spirit within and beyond your group.

C. S. Lewis said, "Christ says, 'Give me All. I don't want so much of your time and so much of your money and so much of your work: I want you. I have not come to torment your natural self, but to kill it. No half-measures are any good. I don't want to cut off a branch here and a branch there, I want to have the whole tree down. Hand over the whole natural self, all the desires which you think innocent as well as the ones you think wicked—the whole outfit. I will give you a new self instead. In fact, I will give you Myself; My own will shall become yours.'"

I pray that you can quit staring through the glass.

I pray you begin daily to ask our great God the three questions, listen to Him respond, and then act on what you hear Him say.

I pray you can grab a hammer and start breaking out of whatever personal or religious fish prison you are in, and live beyond the glass.

Come on out, the water's fine.

Bibliography

Blackaby, Henry T., Claude V. King. *Experiencing God*. 1990.

Bolsinger, Todd. *Canoeing the Mountains*. Downers Grove, IL: InterVarsity Press, 2015.

Curtis, Brent, John Eldredge. *The Sacred Romance*. Nashville: Thomas Nelson, 1997. https://www.amazon.com/Sacred-Romance-Drawing-Closer-Heart/dp/0785273425.

Guindon, Brandon. *Disciple-Making Culture*. Brentwood, TN: HIM Publications, 2020.

Lambert, Mark, Doug Dees. *How God Asks You to Love Others*. Murrell's Inlet, SC: Covenant Books, 2020.

Lewis, C.S. *The Lion, the Witch and the Wardrobe*. New York: HarperCollins Publishers, 1950.

Manning, Brennan. *Abba's Child*. Colorado Springs: NavPress, 1994, 2002.

Mathis, David. *Habits of Grace*. Wheaton, IL: Crossway, 2016.

Stanton, Glen. *The Myth of the Dying Church*. Nashville: Worthy Books, 2019.

Whitney, Donald. *Spiritual Disciplines of the Christian Life*. Colorado Springs: NavPress, 1991, 2014.

IF YOU'RE A FAN OF THIS BOOK, WILL YOU HELP ME SPREAD THE WORD?

There are several ways you can help me get the word out about the message of this book…

- Post a 5-Star review on Amazon.
- Write about the book on your Facebook, Twitter, Instagram, LinkedIn – any social media you regularly use!
- If you blog, consider referencing the book, or publishing an excerpt from the book with a link back to my website. You have my permission to do this as long as you provide proper credit and backlinks.
- Recommend the book to friends – word-of-mouth is still the most effective form of advertising.
- Purchase additional copies to give away as gifts.

The best way to connect with me is by email: dougjdees@gmail.com

ENJOY THESE OTHER BOOKS
BY DOUG DEES

How God Asks You to Love Others
A Field Guide
Mark Lambert and Doug Dees

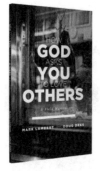

This book is all about you learning to distinguish your voice from God's, so that you can respond immediately when He taps you on the shoulder to do whatever He wants you to do in any of the relationships in your life. We are called to impart to the world around us. Are we ready to be a part of what He wants to do?

reSymbol
A Guide to reThink, reDefine, and reLease the Church
Doug Dees

When you think of church what comes to mind? A steeple? A cross? The unkind reality is this: the way we are thinking about church and operating church is not working as effectively as it could. *reSymbol* exposes some of the symbols that are competing with the visible Christ.

You can order these books from Amazon and Barnes & Noble or where ever you purchase your favorite books.

DOUG IS AVAILABLE FOR COACHING OR SPEAKING.

Contact him at: dougjdees@gmail.com